FOOD, DRINK & TOBACCO I.T.B.

TO A GOOD JOB

The Right Way to a Good Job

by F. J. Taylor

BUSINESS BOOKS
COMMUNICA - EUROPA

First published 1979

© F.J. TAYLOR, 1979

All rights reserved. Except for normal review purposes, no part of this book may be reproduced or utilised in any form or by any means, electronic or mechanical, including photocopying, recording, or by any information storage and retrieval system without permission of the publishers

ISBN 0 220 66364 5

This book has been set 11/12 IBM Baskerville.
Printed in England by T. J. Press (Padstow) Ltd., Padstow, Cornwall,
and bound by Robert Hartnoll Ltd., Bodmin, Cornwall,
for the publishers, Business Books Limited,
24 Highbury Crescent, London N5.

CONTENTS

Preface		*ix*
Chapter 1	**STEP 1: LOOKING AT YOUR SITUATION**	*1*
Chapter 2	**STEP 2: DISCOVERING YOUR TALENTS** Breaking with tradition — Success breeds on itself — Control your future — Dig for your goldmine	*6*
Chapter 3	**CREATING YOUR OPPORTUNITY** Your new aids to success — Examine your standards — Overcoming competition — Selling your talents successfully — Be prepared for change — Successful strategy — Confidence gets results — Use AIDA — Understanding the prospective employer — Surmounting barriers	*16*
Chapter 4	**THE FEMININE ANGLE** The world is your oyster — There's plenty of room at the top — Believe in yourself — Redundancy can open new doors	*37*

Chapter 5	**BEATING THE BARRIER OF THE STANDARD APPLICATION FORM**	*45*
	Know what is behind the application form — Analysing the application form — Success despite the application form — The invaluable resumé — The programme of success	
Chapter 6	**SUCCEEDING AT INTERVIEWS**	*60*
	Planning a successful interview — Concluding a successful interview — Using official sources for help	
Chapter 7	**PROMOTION**	*70*
	Climbing to the top — By-passing the routine job assessment — Keeping vital records — Surmounting promotion obstacles	
Chapter 8	**STAYING AHEAD IN A CHANGING WORLD**	*81*
	Cashing in on change — Achieving success with happiness — Realising your potential — Keeping on top in a changing world — Rising above the average — Harnessing your talents	
Chapter 9	**STARTING YOUR OWN BUSINESS**	*96*
	Pursuing a good idea — Profiting from leisure — Successful preparation — Taking the plunge — Profit from the gap in the market — Conserving your capital — Where to get official help — Operating on a small capital — Profiting from the success of others — Simple rules for success	
Chapter 10	**OVERCOMING STARTING-UP PROBLEMS**	*117*
	Using professional advice — Controlling credit and bad debts — Keeping good business relations — Government	

	regulations — Finding customers — Successful purchasing	
Chapter 11	**BUYING A BUSINESS** Safeguards against failure — Safeguarding the cash — Buying the right shop — Spotting the potential profit — Avoiding loss or theft	130
Chapter 12	**MORE AIDS TO SUCCESS** The success formula — The basic requirements for success — Tax mitigation — Launching an invention — Choosing a profitable shop — Watch your profit margin — Communicating effectively — Money-saving tips — Remunerating salesmen for the best performance — Keeping fit — Safeguarding against failure — Increasing your turnover — Successful expansion — Getting to the buyer	147
Summary		166
Index		169

PREFACE

You want promotion? A better job? So what's stopping you? The simple and brutal answer is that *you* are. Stop blaming anyone else, or the circumstances in which you find yourself. You may even be unemployed through no fault of your own. Perhaps the firm for which you worked closed down, so everyone who worked there, including yourself, became unemployed. What's stopping you getting a new job, and not only a new job, but the kind of job you want? You are.

Don't look around for someone's shoulder to cry on. Don't throw this book into the far corner of the room in disgust. Stop and ask yourself: 'What if he's right? What have I got to do to get where I want?'

First of all, you've got to take a fresh look at yourself and start asking questions. I'll suggest the questions you should ask yourself and, with my guidance, you'll find the answers which will open up a whole new world of understanding for you. Then you can take advantage of unlimited opportunities to advance your career until you reach the top.

What's more, nothing can stop you reaching your goal.

Get one fact firmly fixed in your head. There have never been more opportunities than now to achieve real success.

Even though the number of unemployed is the highest since the pre-war depression days, the world is an oyster to those who make a habit of success.

Being successful is a state of mind reached by paths that can be spelt out very clearly and simply. There is nothing magical or lucky about it. Each one of us has a failure element and a success element built into us from the time we were born. Nobody wants to be a failure, yet only a small percentage of people achieve success and continue to be successful. How do you join this exclusive circle? First and foremost, by understanding yourself totally. Only then can you eliminate the failure factors that prevent you getting that promotion, that better job, or leaving the dole queues and winning the job you really want.

So take a deep breath and make up your mind to take advantage of the steps to success spelt out in this book.

Chapter 1

STEP 1: LOOKING AT YOUR SITUATION

There are four categories of people who are looking for jobs, plus a special type which requires different treatment:

1. The person who has left school, or who will be leaving at the end of the next term and who now has to start looking for a job; and the person who is in a similar position at college or university.
2. The person who wishes to win promotion within his present firm.
3. The person who wants to progress by changing his employment.
4. The person who is unemployed and wants not only a job, but a job that will give him satisfaction and enable him to carve out a career for himself.

And lastly:

5. The person who would like to set up in business for himself and be self-employed.

No matter what category you are in, the basic steps you must take to succeed are exactly the same, and only certain details differ. This book contains many case histories of people who have reached the top in business despite the fact that they had no apparent talents on which to build such successes.

They discovered these necessary talents within themselves,

and you can do the same. One first thing you must thoroughly understand therefore is:

> Don't be one of the crowd. Realise that you have talents and that can get you to the top. Never listen to anyone who tells you that you have no chance to make it.

Let's have a look at someone who is typical of millions of people in this country today. Someone who has had the 'satisfaction' of knowing he has never been out of a job.

Imagine the scene; the works canteen is full of expectant employees. On the platform is a table behind which sits the chairman of the company, flanked by the managing director on his left and the company accountant on his right. A little to one side, covered in embarrassment, sits Bill Smith, clad in a sober business suit, white shirt, with plain tie. His face is red and the sweat stands on his bald head.

The chairman rises: 'Ladies and gentlemen, I am here this afternoon to perform a very pleasant duty to mark the retirement of your colleague, William Smith, who has just completed 30 years as an employee of the firm. After serving in the Army during the last War, Bill — and I hope he will not object to my calling him Bill — joined us in 1947 as a clerk in the accounts department. For the last 20 years he has rendered service to the firm as chief clerk in the accounts department. I am sure you will join with me and my fellow directors in wishing Bill a long and happy retirement, and to mark his loyal and devoted service to the firm over the last 30 years, it gives me very great pleasure to present to Bill this gold watch, suitably engraved.' Handshakes with the directors, clapping from the audience, and dismissal to his suburban home, his garden, pipe, and occasional pint with his cronies at the local.

Now what was your mental reaction to this scene, which is repeated all over the country thousands of times per annum, with variations? Like the majority of his fellow employees, you probably thought: 'There goes a lucky chap. Cushy number for 30 years. Paid off his mortgage on his semi-detached. Must have saved a bit, and should enjoy his retirement.'

What you should have thought was: 'The old fool should have been booed off the stage. Having got himself into a cosy rut, he was content to stop there and become a working cabbage, wasting his talents. With a little bit of effort and determination to make the best of his abilities he could have been sitting where the chairman was, giving out gold watches, instead of receiving one.'

Because he wasn't prepared to think, or use his commonsense, Bill Smith never realised that he had talents which are a highly marketable commodity. With a little bit of planning he could have got promotion after promotion until he reached the chairman's seat, either in his own firm, or elsewhere. So here is the second valuable lesson:

> Provided you have sufficient determination and ability to stick to your objectives through thick and thin, nothing and no one can stop you climbing the ladder of success right to the top.

You may say to yourself, 'Oh yes, it's alright for him to talk, but I've always been unlucky, and there's not much I'm good at. All I seem to do is to make mistakes which stop me progressing, or even getting a job at all.'

If you think like that, whether you are 16 or 60, you are saying that you are right at the bottom, and there's not much you can do about it. But there is hope for you, for if you are at the bottom, there is only one way you can go and that is *up,* and this book will help you to find your talents and get the job you really want and will be good at. Nearly all of us are taught at home, at school, and very often at our first place of work, certain attitudes that limit, or stop, our progress. We are told we are always making mistakes and that we should learn from our mistakes. *Nobody ever learnt anything from their mistakes.* Forget them.

Cash in and make the most of what you are good at, and forget what you are *not* good at. It's your achievements that count, not your failures. Everybody makes mistakes, but the more you dwell upon them, the more mistakes you will make, and the more pain you will give yourself. You will be told you should profit from your mistakes. Have you ever met anyone, let alone yourself, who did? Look at it logically — if you can profit from your mistakes, then surely you should make more mistakes to make more profit? What a load of rubbish! This is an attitude you may have taken for granted, and what I have said might shock you. Good. If it shocks you into realising that what you have always taken for granted doesn't make any sense, then you are making progress. You will progress even faster if you get into the habit of questioning what people say, what tradition dictates, and what you have always taken to be normal attitudes. Think back over your life and you will be surprised and shocked to find how these ideas and traditions have acted against your interests and progress.

Which brings us to your third lesson:

> Break with the old habits and ideas that have been holding you back. Every great advance ever made by man has followed a break with tradition, and you will succeed if you do the same.

If the Wright Brothers had thought like millions of others at that time — 'If man were meant to fly, he would have been born with wings' — they would never have succeeded in building the first machine to fly, the aeroplane. If Sir Isaac Newton had listened to his fellow scholars, he would never have discovered the principle of gravity.

Almost every inventor of note had to fly stubbornly in the face of ridicule and was subjected to a constant barrage of 'It can't be done, give it up, you are a fool to persist'. They proved their critics wrong in the end when their inventions were acclaimed by the world. If inventors had stuck to the ideas and traditions of their time we should not enjoy many of the things we now take for granted such as the electric lamp, radio, television, the telephone, radar, the jet engine, and many more.

Take the case of a man who was written off as a 99 per cent failure. He was given up by his teachers at elementary school as 'hopeless'. After leaving school, he scraped a living as a newsboy. In his late teens he became a telegraph operator on a railway, and a local laughing stock as a 'tinkerer', a man who conducted experiments, all quite useless. However, he refused to give up and shrugged off his critics who were constantly imploring him to stop his foolishness. After every failure he said to himself, 'That's one more experiment I won't have to try'. Then around Experiment 5000, success came to Thomas Alva Edison, for he invented the incandescent electric lamp, and went on to invent dozens of other useful electric devices.

Edison doggedly stuck to his objectives, discarded his mistakes, and promptly forgot them, concentrating on the next step that would lead to eventual success. The great majority of successful inventors, and many successful businessmen, have had to overcome similar obstacles to Edison before they achieved success.

The final lesson in this chapter is, therefore:

>Concentrate all the time on what you know you are best at, and discard your mistakes and failures, for they can only hinder your search for success.

Chapter 2

STEP 2 : DISCOVERING YOUR TALENTS

Your school career might have been classed by your teachers as mediocre, and you may have come to believe they were right, so you didn't try too hard, with the result that when it came to the time you wanted a job, this label of mediocrity stuck with you and you became disheartened to the point where you accepted the apparent fact that you were just 'one of the herd' that were constantly rejected for a decent job. Any job that was offered to you, no matter how menial, would be accepted because you were quite convinced that you had no talents that would justify your applying for a better job.

Philip Fay of Manchester was a lad in this situation. He drifted in a no-hope situation for nearly two years after leaving school, then managed to get an engineering apprenticeship which he took as a last resort. He had decided, after his school career had not brought out any particular talents in him which would be useful in any particular job, that anything would be good enough, so he took the chance of getting an apprenticeship in engineering, although he was not attracted by the trade. After a while he went along to the Worsley Job Centre, to ask the advice of the employment officers. The officer he consulted, Mr Eric Walker, had been a football referee, and whilst questioning Philip about what he really wanted to do, discovered that he was mad about football, and in the previous year had played as a part-timer for Halifax reserves, but they could not afford to sign him on. He told Mr Walker that his ambition had always been to have a career in football ever since he was at school. Mr Walker said he felt he had to try and help Philip who was desperate for a job, so — 'Through my contacts I was able to fix him up with a trial with Anderlecht, the top Belgian soccer club'.

Philip flew out to Belgium and played in a reserve match on the night he arrived. 'I was nervous at first', Philip said, 'but settled down and scored twice. I was getting £29 per week as an engineering apprentice, but Anderlecht are starting me on £80 a week with my board and everything all found.' Three weeks later the club signed him as a full-time soccer professional.

Philip, by a fortunate chance meeting with someone who was prepared to sympathetically consider his case and look beyond a mediocre school career, had discovered that he could cash-in on what he really wanted to do — play football professionally.

Helping yourself

Be concerned with what you want and what you are good at, not with what you don't want. It is customary for people with whom you come into contact for a job, for promotion, for advancement of any kind, to look for what's wrong with you, rather than what's right. They are saying, in effect, 'If he can't make good at one thing, how can he expect to make good at something else, something bigger?'. If you are in a dead-end job, or, because it suits the company's convenience you are in the wrong job and your record in that job is poor, it will be held against you. Here is where you must help yourself. Stop blaming the company and develop ways of showing them how much more effective you can be for the company in another department or section. In this way you are taking control of your own progress to the benefit of both yourself and the company.

Start finding out what you are good at, no matter how useless it might appear to be in helping you along the road to success. Many of our most successful people in all walks of life built their success on talents they had forgotten, or didn't realise they'd got. Some fortunate chance, or the force of circumstance, just like the case of Philip Fay, brought those talents to the fore in their lives, and enabled them to became successful and achieve happiness in what they really wanted to do.

Now you can be master of your own future from this moment on, instead of leaving it to chance to come to your aid. You have talents that can bring you success. In some way or other, since you were a child, you have had some achievements, you have done something that you were good at, even though you and those around you thought nothing of it at the time, or just took it for granted. There is so much that all of us do well and take for granted, never realising that here is something that can reward us with success and happiness.

Sit down quietly somewhere where you won't be disturbed. Have paper and pen ready, and start thinking. 'What do I like to do more than anything else?' 'What have I been good at during my life to this point?' List everything, even the most unlikely things. Things that neither you nor those about you took much notice of at the time. Things you took for granted and enjoyed doing, but which never seemed to further your school, or job career, so you put them out of your thoughts for the future.

Here are some suggestions to start you off. Do you like drawing, or being artistic in any way. Are you musical? Do you like being with animals, or children, or people generally? Are you neat and tidy and like arranging and controlling things? Are you attracted to working with figures, money, facts? Have you a vivid imagination which thinks up situations that appeal to you? Do you gravitate to being the leader in any project or sport? Can you put thoughts and ideas on paper in a readable fashion? Are you naturally humorous? Have you a particularly good memory? Are you observant? Can you organise? Does designing in any shape or form turn you on? Under stress, can you remain calm and decide clearly on ways to overcome the obstacle, or solve the problem? How about selling? Or buying? Does it give you a kick to be of service to people? Do you like playacting and being a showman? Are you good at using words and talking? Have you got a practical mind? Do you like solving problems? Do people turn to you when they are in trouble, or want something done?

You will notice that few of the talents touched on above require eight 'A' levels, or a college degree to show you are good at any of them. The simple fact is that most of our talents, or those things we like to do best, are built into and are a part of our personalities. They only require recognising and developing to achieve the happiness and success. If you have those 'A' levels, or a degree, then you are doubly fortunate, and the world truly is your oyster, if you will only direct your talents to your advantage. It is a pity, and sometimes even tragic, that success in school, college, or university usually means that pressures are put on people to channel their future lives exclusively in the spheres chosen for them by the school, or university counsellor. Usually they are told 'Your 'A' levels (or degree) make you particularly suitable for a career in this or that profession which requires academic achievement in a particular area'. The counsellor's advice is normally drawn from consulting a list of 'suitable' jobs for each category of scholastic success. If the candidate who is seeking advice indicates that he is not interested in following the prescribed path, then the atmosphere usually becomes distinctly cool, and the candidate is classed as a 'rebel' and likely to become a drop-out because he is not prepared to conform to the system. It is unusual to find a counsellor who is prepared to study the achievements of the candidate other than his scholastic successes. Consequently, if the person concerned does not attempt to examine his own deep-felt needs, and looks carefully at what he really likes doing, then he may find himself very unhappy in slavishly following the line recommended by his counsellor. Here, too often are sown the seeds of frustration, instead of personal satisfaction in doing a job at which you can be both successful and happy.

Breaking with tradition

Once you are launched into a job, it is necessary to examine your position continually so that you can recognise the signs of frustration and then be prepared to take energetic action to change to a job, or profession, that will give you more satisfaction because, deep down, you know that is what you want to do. It may mean that you are no better off than you were before, but a job that gives you the satisfaction you want is infinitely preferable to an increase in wages or salary. Moreover, you are more likely to make faster progress in the new environment, because you will be directing your efforts to a better end.

Robin Rippin is the founder and chief executive of Rippon Structures at Auchtermuchty, in Fife, Scotland. He will tell you, 'I'm just a plain laddie' and, to a great extent, he is right. He is the son of a van driver in Fife, his school 'career', if it can be called that, meant that he left school without any qualifications whatsoever, and he was thrown out of his first frustrating job in a garage because he was 'cheeky'. After a time he got a job as a blacksmith for a small agricultural engineering firm. So far, a very ordinary tale which is duplicated by the thousand up and down the country. He has never had any formal education in business, or finance, but whilst he was working for the agricultural engineers, he found he was very interested in welding, drawing designs for steelwork, and working out estimates. Because his interest was aroused, and these jobs gave him great satisfaction, he quickly became very proficient at doing these jobs. After a time he advised the boss to invest in new equipment and expand, but the boss refused to listen to him, so he walked out.

He was determined to use his experience to go it alone. All he had in the bank was £110, but he had a driving ambition to succeed at the job he liked above anything else and at which he knew he was good, so he got the free use of a deserted smithy which was about to collapse and bought a cheap old Gas Board van and a welding machine on hire purchase. He persuaded a supplier to let him have some steel on six months' credit, and his enthusiasm extracted an order from a farmer for a building. For the first month he worked entirely alone, doing his own drawings, cutting up the steel and welding the pieces into prefabricated sections. Whilst he was working on his first order, he managed to get one or two more, so he took on two lads as part-timers working at weekends. By the end of the year he had a staff of six and his drive and enthusiasm had communicated itself to his little team to such an extent that they made and sold nearly £20,000-worth of buildings, with a profit of around £2000.

Then he bought the derelict railway station at Auchtermuchty for a song and converted it into a workshop. Working like a terrier himself, and inspiring the rest of his team, he turns out nearly two tons of prefabricated steel a week, compared with the normal one ton achieved by bigger firms. Such has been his drive and enthusiasm in doing what he wants and enjoying every minute of it, that he now employs over 120 people and has a turnover of more than £1 million. At 38 he must be worth every penny of a million. Whatever happens, one feels, he will continue to succeed in whatever he undertakes. He says, 'I listen to other people and to their advice, but I make up my own mind'.

Success breeds on itself

A strange bonus which is experienced by people like Robin Rippin, who have succeeded against all the odds and have fulfilled all their dreams, even though they started with no apparent advantages, is that their mental ability grows with their progress towards their goal. When people are doing what they like to do best the brain mysteriously responds to this stimulus and provides the answers to all problems which arise from time to time. The capacity of the brain to cope with problems that may appear insurmountable, and for which the person does not seem fitted, is a continual mystery to the experts. They agree there are thousands of cases of this happening all the time, but they cannot put a scientific reason on it. You, as an individual, know that you are 'at your best' when you are doing something you like to do, and your whole being will respond to any challenge or problem you meet *when you are doing what you want to do*. The experts admit this is a factor in human progress which is an uncontrovertible fact. With this knowledge, therefore, you can be assured that *your* brain will cope with any problems you meet, if you are doing a job of work that you like doing.

Take heart and determine that you will discover where your particular talents lie and, with the help of this book, set your foot on the ladder of success with happiness.

Control your future

You should, by now, have started to write down those things you have always enjoyed doing and are good at: your achievements. Dig back into your past and try and remember what you enjoyed then, as well as what you like now. Uncover everything and your list could stretch to as many as ten or a dozen, although that would be exceptional. Don't let false modesty get in your way, or the thought that any outside influence might think you are big-headed. What others thought of your past and present achievements doesn't matter. It's yourself that matters, and it's you who must be in sole and complete control of your future.

Now choose the two talents you have which appeal to you most, the two you feel that you would really like to use in the pursuit of success. These represent the gold you have been digging for. When you know your best capabilities, you will be able to see clearly the paths to the goals you want to reach.

Sometimes we can see talents showing up so strongly in people that we refer to them as born actors, or born salesmen, or born lawyers. These are the people whose outstanding talent was very evident early in life. The violinist who could perform in concert at the age of 7 or 8, the actor who could declaim Shakespeare in the manner born whilst still in his early teens, the salesman who was the outstanding newspaper boy and had other boys working for him, the General who had read all the military books before he was ten. These are the people who were 'destined' to be a success in their chosen career because their outstanding talents would not be denied.

But what about the great majority whose talents are not so easily defined? It is said of many who are successful: 'His achievements came late in life', or that they 'Came as a complete surprise', or 'I didn't know he had it in him'.

The fact is that all these people had those talents present in them very early in life, and what was needed was for themselves, or someone connected with them, to spot their talents and work on them to the advantage of the person concerned. Any success they had achieved later in life could have been reached much earlier if those achievements had been uncovered and exploited.

Now the talents you have can be found and used in so many fields, many of which did not exist even 20 years ago. The opportunities are there to be seized.

There was a boy who plagued his family and relatives with questions like: 'Why does a nail stick to a magnet?' and 'Why does a compass point to the North?' and 'What is magnetism anyway?'. In 1883, his family dismissed these questions with the remark,'Oh, what a nuisance that boy is'. That 'nuisance' was Albert Einstein, who won the Nobel Prize for his theory of relativity at the age of 43. If his incipient genius had been recognised earlier, perhaps he could have made his discoveries many years before.

I cannot emphasise enough, therefore, that it is what *you* consider are the things that are *your* talents and achievements that matter. *Your* opinion is the one that counts, and you can ignore what other people say about you.

Dig for your goldmine

Look at the chap who was a recognised 'success' at 49, a well-respected lawyer at the top of his profession. In all the years he had been in the profession, battling his way to the top, he had resolutely put to the back of his mind that this job did not give him the satisfaction and happiness he really wanted. Just before his 50th birthday he decided he would break away totally from his cosy, well-paid job in the legal profession. He had come to the conclusion that after a quarter of a century on a sure salary and in a comfortable job. He wasn't getting anywhere in achieving personal happiness.

In his school and college life there had been two significant occupations that had given him the greatest satisfaction. One was stamp collecting, and the other was being the advertising manager for the college magazine. Although his parents had objected to his obsession with stamps, telling him he ought to be out with his school friends and joining in with their sports, he had stubbornly stuck to spending his time on his stamp collection, because in no other way could he enjoy himself. When he went to college he took the job of advertising manager and found that he liked meeting people who were potential advertisers and he had no difficulty at all in selling the advertising space. No one else who had held the job previously had achieved anything like the same results.

Why had he finished up as a lawyer after leaving college? He said, 'My parents had always wanted me to be a lawyer, and I took pride in pleasing them'. If it were possible to compile a list of the people whose careers and personal happiness had been ruined or handicapped because a dutiful child followed the dictates of his parents' ambitions, the number would run into millions.

What were the positive values that our friend could discover in his life to this point that could set his feet on the path to personal satisfaction and success in a totally different field from the legal profession? One particular part of his legal job that he did enjoy, and which had played a considerable part in his success as a lawyer, was his ability to settle cases out of court. He had to use a considerable amount of diplomacy and have the ability to negotiate and arbitrate.

But what could stamp collecting add to his store of necessary talents? Quite a few. A dedicated stamp collector has to be highly observant. He has to have an eye for colour and the ability to concentrate in depth on one square inch of stamp more intently than an art connoisseur on an Old Master. Appreciation of design plays a big part in the hobby, as does a wide knowledge of foreign countries. That's a whole range of useful achievements to help him to gain his objective.

Then there was his success as advertising manager of the

magazine whilst he was at college. Here he found that he could get on with a wide variety of people and persuade them to take advertising space in the magazine and that he liked being his own boss and taking decisions.

Once he had dug down into his memory and personality — and he didn't find it easy — and listed his findings, he was three parts along the way to knowing exactly what job he wanted to give him satisfaction, happiness and success. He is now the head of his own large department in charge of foreign and home sales for one of the largest companies in its field. Because of his attention to detail and appreciation of good design he has been able to dress the products up to sell more, brought about improved performance, increased the effectiveness of advertising campaigns and has been able to tackle and understand the complicated laws governing international commerce because of his legal training. His diplomatic ability has enabled him to arbitrate and negotiate successfully, thus keeping his company way ahead of foreign competition.

His summing up is: 'Now I am in a job where I am my own boss, I am having a tremendous amount of fun in doing exactly what I like doing'.

What must be made perfectly clear is that the only advice he took was his own. Discovering the true talents, the 24-carat gold within yourself, is both exciting and tremendously rewarding. You may have been acting a part for so long, either in or out of a job, that sometimes the role you have been playing becomes more real in your mind than your true self. Determine *now* that you will start digging for that true self, for those talents that can achieve everything you want from life.

Chapter 3

CREATING YOUR OPPORTUNITY

In these days of high unemployment, particularly in those places recognised as 'black spots' of unemployment, the person looking for a job goes through three psychological stages. First there is hope that a job can be found, particularly if good school results were achieved. Then follows a period of laziness and no particular desire to work; finally there is a terrifying acceptance that unemployment is all that can be expected and there is no point in trying anymore. If something, anything, eventually turns up in the way of a job, then it is taken, sometimes eagerly, depending upon how long the person has been looking for a job. Often, however, the lethargy into which one has sunk is not easy to shake off, and so one is soon labelled as a 'slacker' and 'not interested in the job', with the result that one is soon back in the dole queue. Once this happens, the slide into deep despondency and resignation to unemployment become inevitable.

This situation is paralleled in the case of the person who is anxious to get promotion in his job, but who finds that all his efforts are blocked by people above him, so finally he becomes disheartened to the point where he sees no point in trying further and becomes firmly convinced that he is not fit for promotion. The only thing left is to spend the rest of his working life in the same job, hoping that the pay will still be adequate for his modest needs. So, day after day, he does just enough to merit retention in his job, just enough to stay on the right side of the bosses.

What you have to do is to create your own opportunity to get where you want. You can dictate your own destiny and ignore conditions around you. Good jobs, the kind of jobs you want, are available in quantity every day, and someone is getting them. Why not you? You do have the qualifications and with those qualifications you can sell your talents to the person who is more than willing to pay well for them.

How do you set about it? You will by now have completed your list of your talents, those things you like doing and which give you the greatest satisfaction. The task now is to marry up those talents to the type of job that can use them to *your* best advantage.

Your new aids to success

To provide a pattern for your task, I will give you three typical examples. First, write down a description of those talents you know you have, then a description of the job you have in mind, with as much detail as you can find from what you have learned about the job.

Example 1

TALENTS

At school I enjoyed being library monitor. I had to keep orderly records of lending and returns. I had to write neatly and I had to meet and deal with a great many people.

I took shorthand and typing lessons at evening classes and also enjoyed the occasional debating sessions as an extra activity.

SUITABLE JOB

Secretary Requirements: accuracy, neatness in taking and transcribing letters, reports, and taking minutes of meetings. Ability to maintain orderly records and files. Dealing with visitors or clients in person or by phone, and poise in meeting a wide variety of people.

MARRYING UP

You like Using words, writing, speaking, filing, organising, being neat and tidy, shorthand and typing, meeting people.

The job wants All the above talents, plus poise and confidence in dealing with people. Because your talents qualify you for all the normal requirements of the job, you will very quickly become confident. Because you are neat and tidy mentally, you will quickly acquire the necessary poise.

   Ah, you will say, that person could do shorthand and typing and could easily get a job as a shorthand typist. Yes, that is very probable, *but,* I didn't marry up her talents with a job as shorthand typist, because she was fitted for the better job of secretary. *Never underrate yourself.* You are selling what is *best in you,* not second best.
   Of course, if you are in a job now as a shorthand typist, you should have no difficulty in getting a good job as a secretary if you have abilities similar to the above.

Example 2

TALENTS

I have always enjoyed dealing with figures. My dad looks to me to supply him with his football perms. Maths was my best subject at school. I liked organising various sports fixtures and had no difficulty in managing the paperwork.

I enjoyed being a Scout patrol leader, creating projects for weekend activities and organising camps for the boys.

SUITABLE JOB

Accountant/Office Manager Requirements: leadership. Ability to organise. Meeting and dealing with personnel. Personnel problem-solving. Systems and procedures. Budgets. Cost controls. Reporting. Ability to handle figures. Orderliness.

MARRYING UP

You like Figurework of all kinds. Organisation. Dealing with paperwork. Leadership. Creating and carrying projects through. Meeting people in all walks of life.

The job wants Just those talents you have. You are ideally situated for these jobs.

But you don't walk into managerial jobs like this straight from school or the unemployment office. True, you can get a job — though the next step up is into the manager's chair. If you are already in an office job, or you are a clerk in an accounts office, then your foot is already on the ladder of success and the next move is up to you. You have got the ability. Create the opportunity.

Example 3

TALENTS

I used to love working with metal in the school workshop. I made several things useful in the home. Dad is a motor mechanic and I enjoyed learning all about the engine of his car. I like the countryside, walking in the hills, studying wildlife and making notes on what I have seen. I can make sketchmaps and enjoy drawing scenes and parts of engines.

SUITABLE JOB

Farm or Estate Management   Requirements: Love of the outdoors. Knowledge of farm machinery. Ability to understand and make large-scale estate maps. Like working with people and animals. Have a strong feeling for the land, crops and trees. Make clear and accurate records. Be able to organise and control the labour force.

MARRYING UP

You like   Working with metal and machinery. Being in the countryside and being interested in everything connected with the outdoors. Sketching, drawing and mapmaking. Walking and outdoor activities.

The job wants   All the talents you have. There are County Agricultural Colleges in every county where you can take a course of farm or estate management, then take a job as a trainee. With your talents you would make a success of the job quickly.

These examples show that experiences which many people would think are of little importance can be used to determine your qualifications for the job you would really like. Some of your talents could be used in a variety of suitable jobs. Following the examples above, you should find it easy to determine which are the must suitable. Setting up a campaign to get that job, or that promotion, or that change of job from one that is unsuitable to one you would like is the next big step.

At this stage it is necessary to issue a warning. Be sure, be very sure, that you are not kidding yourself about your talents. The present education system can be a poor judge of your attainments. An official report recently highlighted this fact. The report, by a joint committee of industrialists and TUC representatives, had this to say: "Pupils with Certificate of Secondary Education passes in mathematics are often unable to do even basic sums when they start work. Employers find that the 'pass' is no guarantee of the youngster's arithmetical competence." They recommended the examination boards to make basic skills a compulsory part of future maths papers. They also recommended that children should be constantly tested in mathematical competence between the ages of 14 and 16.

In another report issued at the same time, the secretary of the Joint Matriculation Board, which examines 125,000 children per year in O-level English, stated that slovenly spelling and gross carelessness amongst its 100,000 candidates who took the last exam had reached 'epidemic proportions'. Thousands of papers verged on total illiteracy and some were 'complete gobbledigook'. Examiners found no sign of any improvement in spelling and punctuation, only a continual deterioration.

Examine your standards

If 'I am good at spelling and/or maths' appears on your list of talents, are you sure your standard is really as high as it must be if you are to make a good impression on your future employer? On the other hand, if you have reached a good standard in these accomplishments, then you have more than a head start in the race for a job over the thousands who are the subjects of the reports above. Make no mistake, once you are confronting a potential employer any shortcomings will soon become very evident, and your chances of getting where you want will quickly melt like snow in summer.

Even if you don't include these particular basic skills on your list, it will pay you to make sure that you are reasonably competent in both, because they play an important part in practically any job you are trying to get.

The great majority of those people looking for a job know

of nothing better than the standard procedures. Register at the local employment office and wait until you are sent for an interview. Scan the 'situations vacant' columns in the newspapers. Tout your friends to ask if there are any jobs going in their firm. It is a fact that where the job is in a machine shop, on a production line of any description, or the work is simple and requires little training, then a large proportion of jobs that occur are taken by relatives and friends of those already employed in that firm. Thousands of men have followed their fathers into car factories or down the mine. Millions of girls have joined their relatives and friends on the packing line of a manufacturer. This is an easy way that an employer will use to fill his vacancies and with little danger of being let down. The employer knows that any employee who has introduced a relative or pal on to the line is going to make quite sure that the new fellow, or girl, isn't going to let them down. This is unfortunate for the deserving person who would like such a job, but has no personal recommendation, but it is a fact of life that an employer will take the easy way, provided it's a safe way, of taking on new labour.

The new Employment Protection Act doesn't help either, for there are thousands of cases where a person who has been given employment has been sacked for what the employer considers perfectly good reasons, and has then gone to the Tribunal and been awarded a large sum for being 'unfairly' sacked. If the employer appeals it will cost him a great deal of money to overturn the decision of the Tribunal, so every employer is very wary of taking on new staff who are totally unknown to him or his employees. You have to present him with a case that he must look at and be very reluctant to turn down. The sour realities that have to be faced by every genuine person looking for a job who is prepared to play fair with his new employer is that an Act which was intended to protect those in employment from being unfairly dismissed should now be an instrument contributing to continuing unemployment.

The provisions of the Act are an open invitation to anyone who has been dismissed for any reason, whether justified or not, to apply to the Tribunal for a case to be made against his late employer for unfair dismissal. Even though the case against the employer is thrown out, and the dismissal upheld by the Tribunal, it has cost the employer a considerable amount of valuable time and money to contest the case. Whether justified or not, employers generally are convinced that the Tribunals are biased against them, and they are judged to be guilty before they are proved innocent. More and more employers are opting for a settlement out of court, even though they are perfectly certain the dismissal of the employee was 100 per cent justified. Whatever happens, therefore, the employer loses out. The bosses of thousands of small companies would prefer not to expand sooner than take on new staff who might cost them a great deal of money, which they can ill-afford if they have to dismiss anyone for what they regard as unsatisfactory conduct. It has been stated by many official bodies connected with industry that, if it were not for this almost universal fear small company bosses have, the unemployment figures could be reduced very considerably if each of the small companies took on just one more person.

Bear this in mind when approaching a propective employer and impress him with your willingness to play fairly by him. It may be one of the biggest hurdles you have to overcome in your search for the job you want.

Competition

A hurdle equally as big is the competition you have to face in getting a job. With high unemployment and many other people scrambling for the job, employers can afford to be very choosy about whom they take on. The standards they look for are far higher than a few years ago when the position was reversed, and jobs were there for the asking. The same situation applies over promotions. More people hang on to their jobs and are reluctant to change because of the difficult employment situation, so your path to promotion within your firm is blocked for much longer than it would have been in the past. To progress therefore it is *you* who must change your job.

All these factors present you with the opportunity you have been looking for, strangely enough. With your credentials, the case you have constructed highlighting your talents, your particular fitness for the job *you* have chosen, you and your talents will stand out like a beacon on a mountain. The prospective employer must sit up and take notice, because here at last he is faced with something that is different from the usual tired ordinariness. He expects to meet incompetent, ill-prepared candidates all the time, for that seems to be the norm at present.

You and your case will be like a strong beam of sunlight breaking through a dull day, and he will be eager to listen to you. You are the one with the initiative, you will ensure that the interview proceeds along the lines you have mapped out, you will guide the person you are facing back on to your path if he shows signs of straying.

It is a horrifying fact that thousands of candidates for a job never bother about their dress, or bearing, when they apply for a job. It just does not occur to them that anyone slovenly dressed, or who slouches into the interview room, probably with hands in pockets, even with a cigarette dangling from the corner of his mouth, has damned his chances of getting the job from the moment he walks into the room.

Selling your talents successfully

To get the job you want you must sell yourself and your talents to the prospective employer. The selling method differs little from any successful method of selling any commodity. There is a well tried formula known to most salesmen: AIDA — four steps to a successful sale.

A   *Attention*   You must get the attention of your prospect.
I   *Interest*   You must get his interest.
D   *Desire*   You must arouse his desire to buy what you are selling.
A   *Action*   You must persuade him to take action and give you the order.

Anyone buying subconsciously follows this sequence.

If you are buying household items in a shop, you are attracted to the item which is packaged to catch your eye. If goods packed in a plain dull box are on a display shelf next to a similar item attractively wrapped, your automatic reaction is to choose the pack that catches your eye. Each year, millions of pounds are spent on designing and producing packaging that will induce sales. It is a well known fact that many cosmetics and allied products are in packages that cost considerably more than the contents. Notwithstanding that fact, if the manufacturers doubled the contents and put them up in a plain pack with a plain label, they just would not sell. A costly, beautiful package that catches the attention better than its competitors is the one that will sell the product. If it is being offered to the public for the first time, then it has to promote interest in the choosy buying public, and generate a desire to at least try it. This is done through advertising in its many forms. The large companies will spend millions of pounds on advertising to launch a new product successfully. Many large, and some smaller, companies will willingly lose money for the first year in the hope that they can recoup their very large expenditure by sales which prove the product a success.

Then comes the biggest test of success. Following the first purchase, will the fickle public buy again? Will they continue to buy it? Having been persuaded by the advertising and the attractive package to try the product, will the contents come up to their expectations? Will they say to themselves, 'Gosh, that was good, I'll certainly buy that brand again'. If more than 50 per cent of the original buyers repeat their purchase, then the product is reckoned to be a huge success.

So, all the four steps of AIDA have been successfully taken. The package has aroused attention, usually triggered off by the advertising, which in turn has aroused interest. Advertising and the package have combined to promote the desire to try the product. Finally, the manufacturer has made certain that the contents are of the best quality, ensuring the repeat sales and loyalty to his product by the buying public. The promotion has finally achieved the desired end — action by the public in buying the product.

It doesn't stop there of course. Right through the life of that product, until it is superseded by something else, its sales must be continually promoted, and its packaging and contents continually improved to keep it ahead of its competitors.

With you as the product, and your prospective employer in the place of the purchaser of the product, the procedure is exactly the same. You have to get the attention of the employer. You can make your personality felt by the way you get the interview, then get his full attention the minute he sets eyes on you before you have opened your mouth. Looking for, and recognising, the signs of his favourable attention, you then arouse his interest in your talents — your previous achievements. Putting your case across in the right manner must make him desirous of trying your talents out in his firm. So he takes the action for which you planned and agrees to give you a trial. You have created such an impression on him that he is congratulating himself upon his acumen in giving you a trial. He has subconsciously ensured that he will take a special interest in your progress personally. It is now up to you to be very sure you don't let him down. If he, or any other employer, is to continue to 'buy the product', i.e. help you up the ladder to success, you must continually increase the efficiency of your work and personality. Only by these means will you ensure that you are the first to be considered in any promotion, or that you can be certain of getting that better job in another firm. Don't kid yourself that you can rest on your laurels, or that you are so good your employer must recognise your worth automatically. It doesn't happen. You can't afford to let up if you want to get to the top. You must always be one step ahead of the herd, always alert to the opportunities that constantly occur of taking the next step up the ladder.

Be prepared for change

Bear something else in mind. Statistics show that the people who get to the top quickest do not get there by staying in one firm. They are aware that jobs are going all the time in the next stratum of jobs above their own, and they are continually preparing themselves to apply for, and get, such a job. It may seem disloyal to your present employer who may have been particularly good to you, but it is usually the only way to get where you want to be, in the time you have mapped out for yourself. No matter how good an employer is, he will not, unless you show exceptional brilliance, promote you over the heads of good existing people, and waiting to step into dead men's shoes is not the way to mount the ladder in *your* time scale.

Remember, too, that by leaving your present situation, you have made a vacancy for someone else to step into, for which they will be grateful. If you wish to progress, accept that change is an essential part of your long-term plan and that each change you make creates an opportunity for someone else. Dismiss any thoughts of disloyalty, or any idea that you are deserting a good employer and leaving him in the lurch. There are always capable people ready to take your old job, and any reasonable employer knows that he has no right to try and stop an ambitious person from moving on and climbing higher. His satisfaction lies in the knowledge that you have given of your best whilst you were in his employment, and he has profited thereby. You have been a a very good investment whilst he employed you, and it is up to him to make sure that the person who steps into your shoes is just as good an investment.

The first step in your plan is to get an interview with the boss, or personnel manager, of the firm you'd like to work for. If you can, make a list of six or more such firms. Find out who the top man is. This isn't difficult. You've got a tongue in your head, and anyone who already works for the firms you have chosen will give you the name of the boss. *Always* make your approach to the boss, *not* to anyone below him if you can possibly avoid it. If, after seeing the top man, he refers you to the personnel manager for him to go into details, that's OK, but a referral from the boss himself will ensure the cooperation from the personnel manager that you want.

That's a pretty tall order, you may say. I can hardly expect a busy boss to give me an interview just on my say-so.

Perfectly true, but your plan has no room for the ordinary, difficult, and sometimes impossible approach. Send a letter to each of the people you have listed. I mentioned six as a minimum, but the more you can list the better. Up to 100 if you like.

Here are some suggestions on the content of the letter:

---

1   If you are looking for your first job

Dear Sir,

I am looking for information to help me in my career. It's not the kind of information I can get from just anybody, and that is why I am approaching you. In brief, I would like to know if there may be a need for someone with my qualifications in the (town or district) area. I am not asking you for a job. All I want is your commonsense opinion as a business leader. I feel that your advice, backed by good business judgement, will be very helpful when I start looking for a job. Here in brief is my background. (List your accomplishments. Just state them simply witnout any attempt at embellishment.)

If you think there may be a demand for someone with my qualifications in the area, I would appreciate your advice as to whether it would be best to approach individual companies personally, or to send them a resumé of my educational career that might open up employment possibilities in advance.

Your opinion and advice would be very much valued,
I look forward to hearing from you,

Yours sincerely,
(Your signature)

2   *If you are looking for a change to a better job*

Dear Sir,

I am looking for information to help me in my career. It's not the kind of information that I can get from just anybody in helping me to come to the right conclusion. All I want is your commonsense opinion as a business leader. In brief, I would like to know if there may be a need for someone with my qualifications in the (town or district) area. I am not asking you for a job as I already have a good one, but I do wish to improve my position. Here in brief is my background: *(List your background as above)*.

If you think a demand for someone with my qualifications might occur in the future, I would appreciate your advice as to whether it would be better to make a personal approach to individual companies, or to send a resumé to as many as possible in this field.

Your opinion and advice would be greatly appreciated, and I look forward to hearing from you.

Yours sincerely,
(Your signature)

It should hardly be necessary for me to emphasise that these letters must be in your own handwriting, *not* typed, that your writing is neat and legible, your spelling correct, and that you use the best type of paper and envelope you can afford. Remember, it's the first impression that counts. Start your address on the envelope with: 'For the personal attention of Mr XXX (the executive's name)'. Enclose a stamped addressed envelope for a reply.

Statistics indicate that about four out of ten people reply, and that should give you plenty to work on. Usually the letters will be somewhat formal, stating that you would be welcome to call and have a word with the writer. You aren't likely to be offered a job, for you didn't ask for one. You may remark 'What's the point? I want a job, and all I get is advice.'

Successful strategy

The answer to that question is 'strategy'. If you ask directly for a job or a trial in his firm, his automatic reaction is 'No' as his first line of defence. You become a supplicant, asking him for a big favour. His second reaction is one of resentment. 'What's this person bothering me for? Especially as I have no vacancies.' Finally he will probably think, 'If this person wants a job, that's his problem, not mine. I've got enough of my own problems without taking on his as well.'

If by chance you do get a reply to your letter asking for a job, you can bet your boots it will be on these lines: 'With your qualifications you should have no difficulty getting a job. I'll keep you in mind and if anything comes up in the future I'll let you know.' Politely, you have been told to get lost in no uncertain terms.

On the other hand, when you ask a man for advice, you compliment his good judgement. He starts taking a personal interest in you. Writing to him for advice, and nothing else that will commit him, marks you as someone with initiative and good sense. If he gives you his advice, he will be anxious to know how you get on. He will be pleased to give you names of people and firms who would give you an interview.

To everyone who replies to your letter, acknowledge immediately with a follow-up on these lines:

Dear Sir,

Thank you for your helpful advice. I am sure you will wish to know how I progress, and I will be pleased to keep you informed.

                                          Sincerely yours
                                          (Your signature)

You won't expect a reply to that acknowledgement and it's very unlikely you will receive one. Wait about a month then send another letter to all those who replied in the first place. Something like this:

Dear Sir,

Following your helpful advice, I am now well prepared to look for a suitable job. I would like to take the opportunity of thanking you in person and will telephone you in a day or so, hoping that you can spare me a few minutes. If in the meantime you do know of anyone who might have an opening, I would be glad of your recommendation following our meeting.

With many thanks,

Yours sincerely
(Your signature)

Confidence gets results

You must prepare yourself for a successful meeting by knowing all your capabilities perfectly, and being able to speak or write about them effectively and enthusiastically at an interview. Let your confidence in yourself show through to anyone you may meet. Do not be hesitant or apologetic over any point that might be raised. If there is a question about anything that you can't answer, don't try and flannel round it; say you haven't the knowledge to answer that particular question. Never be 'cheeky', or over-demanding, just be straightforward and factual. A confident smile will get a far better reaction than a worried look.

Remember that your first meeting with the first 'boss' who agrees to see you may not even reach the point of talking about a job. He will be intrigued to see this person who made such an unconventional approach, and the few minutes he can spare to see you will probably be taken up with talking about subjects quite unrelated to the main subject. You will, none the less, be the object of a pretty shrewd summing-up whilst this chat is going on.

If you have made a good impression, he will probably ask you to tell him about yourself, and you must be ready for that. If you have several accomplishments, or talents, ask him which you should start with. Mention the two or three which you know are your best and on which you are best qualified to speak with authority, but without bragging. He will probably leave the choice to you. Make it as brief as possible, but make it good. Be confident and let the executive be in no doubt that you are in command of the subject.

For instance, if you are looking for a better job than the present one you hold as an office manager: 'In the field of office systems analysis, I reorganised our systems, procedures and flow of work. I found there were various weekly and monthly reports which had little meaning, so these were dropped. Other paperwork I was able to reorganise so that the operation became much simpler whilst being more effective. The staff were able to cope better, the job was speeded up, and as staff left, or retired, there was no need to replace them. In less than two years the job was much more effective and efficient, and the staff had been cut by 25 per cent.'

In less than two minutes you have given the main facts which could not fail to impress the person listening. No reason for flannel, or 'dressing the facts up'. Your achievements spoke very clearly for themselves.

If you have your listener's whole interest at this point, he may suggest that you give him a resumé on your other accomplishments.

Use AIDA

In your preparation for these interviews, and whilst they are proceeding, always remember our selling formula AIDA. You have now succeeded in getting the boss's attention and interest. The impression you have made on him will lead easily to his desire to help you further and to take action to make that help meaningful. At no point has an actual job been discussed, but his action may take one or more of several specific paths, all designed to help you in your search for the job you want. He may refer you to his personnel manager, telling you that although he knows there aren't any jobs going in his firm at the moment, he is sure that the manager would like to meet you and, probably, that this person can inform you about possible vacancies in other companies. The boss will make certain that the manager is aware that you are in a different class to the usual, run-of-the-mill applicant.

Personnel managers are hard-bitten types who can see through phonies very quickly, and they are trained to spot where you are good, where you are not so good, and where you are lousy. He will very likely give you a gruelling interview, and if he is still impressed at the end of it he will be more than willing to refer you to other personnel managers. At no time have you asked for a job, and so you have not embarrassed the influential people you have met. This should be your strict pattern as you see each executive, or manager, in a series of interviews. Each meeting adds to your experience and brings you more influential friends who are anxious to help you. At some point, you are going to be asked to consider applying for a job which is open and is of the calibre for which you are looking. Your plan has worked. You have achieved your success through your own efforts and proved that you truly are the 'master of your fate'.

Your plan of campaign should have more than just one option. Whilst the method I have advocated in this chapter should achieve your goal, do not neglect the more conventional methods of seeking a job. Many very good jobs are advertised in both national and local newspapers, or trade papers. The employment offices maintain a jobs index of situations vacant all over the land. Where you can gain the advantage over competition for these jobs is through your planning, selling yourself and your accomplishments, making certain that an interview is governed by you, and steered in such a way that you make a greater impression on your interviewer than the other candidates.

Understanding the prospective employer

Most executives, or personnel managers, who have a good job to be filled are in an uncomfortable spot when they interview people. You may think that it is the person who is applying for the job who is in the hot seat and who has to pit his poor wits against an ice-cold professional interviewer, but he is in a worse position than you. Because the interview takes place in his office he has to play many parts. He has to offer a welcome to someone who may be a welcome guest, or an awkward adversary. Whilst he has to be the boss, because he has the power of saying 'yes' or 'no', with a finality that may dash a candidate's hopes completely, or offer him a bright future, he has to be friendly in order to encourage the applicant to talk freely about himself and supply the information required. He has to 'sell' the job, without committing himself to buy the talent that is being offered for sale. In the short time available for each interview he has had to play many parts. Host, boss, inquisitor, friend, psychologist, potential buyer, encourager, continually changing his role. All the time he has had to maintain an attitude of pleasant fellowship whilst mentally trying to reach a cool impartial decision that might make or break the applicant.

Surmounting barriers

He also has the haunting fear that he might make a wrong choice, as the person who gets the job might turn out to be quite unsuitable. This means that his choice is in question, he 'loses face' with his bosses, and the whole wretched business of finding the right person has to start all over again. There is no wonder therefore that so many firms have preferred to let soulless 'application forms' weed out their applicants for them, followed by standard intelligence and aptitude tests to reduce the number further. If the results weren't always perfect, at least they spared the executive or manager the ordeal of passing judgement personally on the applicant. As one executive said, voicing the thoughts of thousands of his fellow executives: 'I can buy our raw material and sell our finished product as well as the next chap, and drive a pretty hard bargain, but buying a person's career is a very different kettle of fish. I feel like a slave-dealer, poking a finger into someone's head to see if there is anything there.' The unfortunate effect these standard procedures have is that they reduce every applicant to the status of an automaton or robot with no personality of their own, and it gives an automatic bias towards the person who can be glib and slick when filling in forms. They are often the people who comprise the final few who are actually interviewed personally by the boss or personnel manager. If the job for which you are applying entails going through these procedures, fill in the form or forms in a very careful way, making sure your writing and spelling is good, which will ensure a good impression is made. The 64,000-dollar question is: 'How can I jump one step ahead of the rest and be pretty certain I can be in at the final interview'.

Compose a note attached to the form stating that whilst you appreciate the necessity of the form, and you have filled it in to the best of your ability, you feel that your accomplishments are such as to merit a personal interview which will enable you to present your valid case far better than a form can. Either separate from, or combined with such a note, you can find out the name of the executive who is in charge of the final interview and talk to him on the phone emphasising the strength of your request for an interview. He can't shoot you down in flames, and it's far more likely he will admire your initiative and enterprise and grant you what you want.

Prepare yourself very carefully for the interview if you are successful in getting one. The executive will be looking forward with keen interest to see what kind of person you are. He will have built up a mental image of you that is favourable but potentially very critical, because he may well have it at the back of his mind that you might have 'conned' him into giving you an advantage over your fellow applicants. He will start by giving you the benefit of the doubt, but it is up to you to make quite certain that the impression he gets during the interview is totally favourable, and that you leave him in no doubt at all that it was worth spending his valuable time in seeing you. You might get quite a grilling; you must expect this and be ready for it for you are laying your future on the line. Pass this barrier successfully and the world is your oyster, but never regard interviews such as this as a contest between a potential employer and yourself, with you as the attacker and him as the defender. Your whole plan must be based on a friendly, open relationship without any attempt to score points over an 'adversary'. After all, if you are offered a job, you will want to maintain a friendly status with the person who is now your boss. Aggression in an interview is hardly likely to prove successful in getting the job. It is your calm, confident bearing and factual presentation of your well-thought-out case that will achieve the goal you seek, and leave the competition groggy.

Chapter 4

THE FEMININE ANGLE

Oil rigs are one of the few areas of heavy industry still denied to women. A girl recently tried very hard to become the first woman working as a miner at the coalface. Apart from these areas and one or two more where sheer brawn is the principal asset, women now perform tasks in sectors of industry where, until quite recently, the mere idea of employing women would have been laughed to scorn. Women now drive heavy vehicles on long-distance journeys, operate successfully in the construction industry, and drive public service vehicles. In John Carr's woodyard in Doncaster, it's the women who do the heavy jobs. The men mind the machines, whilst the women — 400 of them — physically move heavy doors, windows and large cases of planks, plus the job of converting the planks into doors, windows and other construction woodwork — a combination of building labourer and carpenter. Frances Towle, now pushing 60, has been there since 1943, when women had to take the place of the men. The system has survived because sufficient men are not available to do the work. Men want the joinery work where they can earn a lot more money. 'You can't get the men to flog like we flog', said a fragile 4'10" girl who spent most of her time lifting firecheck doors weighing a hundredweight, amongst other heavy jobs. 'The men could do the job, but not at the speed. After a time a man gets tired, but so long as we get our cup of tea, we carry on at the same fast rate.' Mrs Castle said: 'We've done some pretty heavy jobs here at Carr's. At one time we were making whole house fronts.'

Visitors to the works of Herbert Morris Limited, at Loughborough, could be forgiven for thinking their eyes were deceiving them when they look at the driver of the huge gantry crane and see a pretty blonde delicately handling the job of moving immense steel girders with tremendous precision. Training instructor Alan Newton says: 'As far as crane driving skills go, the women beat the men always. They are amongst the best we've got. They work beautifully in phased team work which demands a high degree of skill and coordination and, unlike some of the men we have had, they don't make mistakes.'

Beverley Jocelyn decided she had had enough of a clerk's job and muscled her way into a job driving a 45-ft articulated lorry. She says: 'I went straight from a £20-a-week job as a clerk to earning £80 a week on the motorway. I do exactly the same job as the men, loading my own vehicle, and the 40-ft trailer. Loading, roping and sheeting is a heavy job and needs a lot of physical hard work, but I hold the job down successfully. It gave me a tremendous feeling of freedom just to go out and do the job on my own.'

The world is your oyster

Schoolgirls still think that the range of jobs open to them is confined largely to nursing, shop assistant, clerk, and all the other jobs that are traditionally 'women's work'. They envy the boys whose imagination can range from being a pilot to deep-sea diving around the oil rigs. Those girls and women who have had the courage and nerve to break out into what has previously been an exclusive man's world have shown that they can perform these jobs as efficiently as the men — and sometimes better. With a million and a half unemployed are these opportunities really there? John Fraser, Junior Minister of Employment, said: 'There is a gross shortage of skilled people in many areas. In some development towns factories are closing because they can't get the workers. Women should abandon the idea of unskilled employment and get themselves skilled. Training is available.'

Women can use as much courage as a man in becoming competent and skilled. The three vital 'Ps' can help you get where you want — Perseverance, Patience and Pluck. Determine what you want to do, make your plans and persistence will see to it that you reach your goal.

Although the Equal Opportunities Commission officially put paid to prejudice against women when seeking jobs in competition with men, such prejudice still flourishes in many quarters, although now illegal. Prejudice sits very comfortably on a man's shoulders, like an old coat, and it is very difficult to persuade him to change an old, ingrained attitude that has been there for centuries. Without his old comfortable coat he feels very exposed and vulnerable. He will retreat into a bastion of excuses, such as, 'A woman is not suited for this type of job because she is too weak, or hasn't the stamina', or 'The men won't work alongside a woman'. Rubbish, and it's up to you to prove it's rubbish by emphasising your suitability. In the last resort, the potential employer will try and grade you below the men doing a similar job, and pay you less. This is where you must take a very firm stand, and there are many officials connected with the employment offices, careers offices and government agencies who will come to your aid.

Notwithstanding these official bodies who should be on your side, it is often the most satisfactory way to get what you want, and the quickest, to prove to your employer that you are worth the same money as a man. He will bolster his prejudice with one or more of a number of excuses. 'A man has a family to support, whilst a woman has only herself to consider.' 'A woman is subject to more health hazards than a man, and is likely to have more time off.' Rhubarb. Pure unadulterated excuses born of old-time prejudice. Let your talents speak with no uncertain voice and show him that not only are you worth a man's pay, but that is what you are going to get. Make no mistake, many women who have taken this stand are being paid the rate for the job, and sometimes more. On the stage, in the film world, in advertising, in fashion, journalism, administration, management, and politics, women are proving all the time that they can compete with, and often better, the performance of men. No reason therefore why you shouldn't break through this barrier of privilege for men and claim your just rights, *because you are worth it!*

There's plenty of room at the top

Louise Peachey, one of the few women stockbrokers in Britain, explains how she got to the job in a profession previously regarded as exclusively a man's world. "I left school with five 'O' levels and took a secretarial course. I took a job as secretary to an advertising executive. When he was away I did all his work. It was suggested that I become an accounts executive, but the boss turned it down. He said that if I were a man the job would have been mine, but women don't become account executives. 'Why not', I asked. 'Because the job is to put the client at ease. With a woman in charge, if the clients like you they'll want to go to bed with you, and if you don't fall in with their wishes, they won't like you.' The situation became farcical, so I kept changing jobs, then signed on as a 'temp' at a bureau. One of the temporary jobs I got was working for a director of a merchant bank. I thoroughly enjoyed that and I gave myself a year to find an executive position dealing in stocks and shares. In ten months I secured a job. It was worth all those interviews where I knew they didn't really want me as an employee, but where they were fascinated by this crazy woman who thought she could be a stockbroker. When I first went in my new capacity to a buffet lunch given by a large insurance company, I had to take a deep breath as I was the only woman there. Men daren't come near me in case their colleagues talked! So, instead of being surrounded when I walked into the room, as I'd expected, I was left strictly alone. Having passed my exams, I braved the Stock Exchange floor on the first day it was open to women. The men stared, but I wasn't at all frightened. My partners were — they had to go and console themselves with a bottle of champagne!

"I think my determination and persistence counted for a

lot. Because I didn't have any 'A' levels, I had to study economics and monetary theory at night school. You don't need to be man to do this job. All you need is a pleasant personality and a good memory."

Liz Calder, who is now an editorial director of a well known publishing house, says she suffered from a lack of direction when she was a child and it wasn't until she was 30 that she decided to break out into having a go for better things. She had a post in the publicity department, took a deep breath and managed to move to editing, which is very rare for women. It was a comparatively easy step to the position of director once her talents were recognised.

She says she sees too many girls coming into publishing as secretaries, and often they are only doing someone else's typing, which is a dead-end. They have the unfortunate female characteristic — they are not prepared to push themselves. Young women often lack confidence because no one has encouraged them. 'I've found I can do things I was scared of, simply by taking the plunge and having a go.'

Believe in yourself

Mary Overton has been running her own employment agency for some time and finding jobs in the executive class is one of her principal tasks. Her experiences reveal a great deal about the problem. She tells the story of a woman who came to her not so long ago, and who had very good qualifications. 'I got her an interview with the managing director of a company and he offered her the job of marketing manager. Then she came back to Mary to discuss terms. "Do you know", Mary said, 'She said to me as soon as she came in, 'Do you *really* think I'm capable of doing that job? Am I *really* up to it?' I was furious with her. When it comes to the crunch, few women will believe they are as good as men, and it's time they started standing up for themselves."

If a man is interviewed for a job and is asked about his qualifications, he will expound upon his talents, working experience and skills; not, like many women, on his personality and a vague idea of his merits. Girls, unlike boys, are not programmed for a life of work and success. It is taken for granted that work will only occupy a part of their lives, with marriage as their main object in life, so they tend to approach a job with an attitude which is often frivolous. Because their main ambition is to marry and have children, any job they have prior to marriage is just a fill-in to keep them happy until some lucky chap meets up with them at the altar.

Marriage, children, *and* a good job are regarded as incompatible, even impossible. Women *have* adjusted to this situation, and I don't mean the women who have to spend eight hours a day at a menial job to augment their husband's small income and keep their children well fed and well clothed. Many women in that situation would give their right arm to spend all their time at home with their children. A man who is ambitious is praised and envied by his compatriots, but a woman who is ambitious and successful is regarded as somewhat of a freak, particularly if she is happily married with a family. She should be looked on with awe as a marvel who has successfully planned her life to give her and her family the best of all worlds. Such women are to be found in every sector of the professions — doctors, lawyers, estate agents, self-employed, and in industry in many types of managerial jobs.

The growing demand by women looking for a decent career, to be recognised as being equal to men in their ability to hold a good job down successfully, is making slow progress in some areas. In others, prejudice against women still reigns. The Ashridge Management College has commissioned an investigation into the reason why the proportion of women managers to the whole workforce is not rising at the same rate as the proportion of women workers. Senior male managements still believe that it is not cost-effective to train women in management, 'Because they stay for a maximum of five years'.

Ashridge say that they have definite proof that women managers stay for an average of 10 years. Training, therefore, makes economic sense. The Chemical and Allied Products Industry Training Board have realised that 'There must be something wrong if, in an industry with over 50 per cent women employees, only 5 per cent of the managers are women'. They have started a business management training scheme for women. This year, 1978, they hope to sponsor 16 women and 'start to establish a tradition of women in senior management'. The Equal Opportunities Commission is working on a plan to get the Civil Service to reduce their entry age for women who wish to enter the executive officer grade, from 28 to 20 with two 'A' levels. The fact that gradually more opportunities are opening up for women is getting through to the women themselves. Thirty-two per cent more women chose business management degrees in universities in 1977 than in 1976. Unfortunately careers advisors at school still stick to the old and hackneyed narrow range of 'jobs suitable for girls'. Although the Engineering Industry Training Board are actively sponsoring training for girls and women and advocate them taking technical apprenticeships, everyone concerned complains about the lack of support from schools, yet the shortage of technicians is crucial and the choice of jobs enormous. The outlook for the 100 girls taking a 2-year training through the Industry Board sponsorship is bright in the extreme, but girls are entering for this training *despite* careers advice at school and not *because* of it.

Redundancy can open new doors

Redundancy is the one big fear that haunts the woman who supports herself, particularly if she is 40-plus and has a good job with a good life style to match. Pam Horner went through this devastating, traumatic experience. She began her career as a secretary and her talents eventually won for her the job of a top executive in an advertising agency. Then, in her 40s, the company folded and all the employees from the managing director downwards were made redundant. All of them then started feverishly scanning the advertisement pages of the trade press and the national newspapers for suitable jobs to apply for.

Her experiences and the way she won through to another good job should provide a good example for all women who find themselves in a similar unfortunate and totally unexpected position. She explained: 'You learn quickly enough when applying for jobs by the score that your curriculum vitae isn't enough. You have to prepare several accounts of your experience, tailoring them specially to the particular job and prospective employer you are approaching. There is a definite art in applying, I assure you. I think this is why the government's Professional and Executive Recruitment Scheme isn't working very well. You have to give your work history on a soulless form which goes into a central computer, and when firms are looking for staff, they contact PERT and get the list, but it isn't geared to anything for every applicant is reduced to a statistic. I had no one to cushion me from the financial realities of my position. I had some savings but quickly realised how soon these disappear when there is no income. The dole money was welcome but pathetic, coming nowhere near keeping me solvent from week to week. Being redundant had an oddly paralysing effect. I daren't plan a holiday, invite people to stay, or even go to a theatre. I half wondered if I would have to sell my home in order to survive.

'Having been a secretary in the old days, I suppose I could have stifled my pride and found a job there, but I took a good hold on myself and determined that the job level I had reached before redundancy was the level I was going to stay in. Then I made painstaking preparations for applying for the job I now have — deputy director of the Advertising Standards Authority. Three interviews and three months later I was awarded the job. I was flattered to learn that 300 people had applied for the job. Knowing I had come out top and got the job restored my ego which undoubtedly had taken a knock.' Pam need not have been so modest. She planned to get the job, set about the task with a determination that she maintained through three interviews and emerged as the winner of a contest with 300 trailing behind. If you find yourself in this situation, emulate Pam Horner and get the job *you* want.

What Goethe said in one of his poems a century and a half ago still holds good today:

> Whatever you can do, or dream you can, begin it.
> Boldness has genius, power and magic in it, *Begin it now!*

Chapter 5

BEATING THE BARRIER OF THE STANDARD APPLICATION FORM

The refuge of the 'Standard Application Form', behind which so many managements hide when they are offering jobs, is a difficult hurdle any applicant has to face. In every corner of the country miles and miles of files are cluttered up with completed application forms, like gravestones in a cemetery commemorating the death thousands upon thousands died when they committed their future to this soulless monster.

Why do executives and boards of directors do it? When questioned, they will say, 'We know it has its serious shortcomings, but it's the best we can do to find suitable applicants and to weed out the deadwood. We know of nothing better, and we've got to have something.'

The standard form is a masterpiece compiled by a statistician, and the disaster is often compounded by a computer. Forms full of little boxes which have to be filled in with the same old ticky-tacky information which is mostly quite useless. How can a genuine applicant, who would be a gem of an employee, get across his hopes and ambitions, his personality and talents, those real achievements worth a pot of gold to the potential employer? One employer admitted he regarded these completed forms as 'the agony file'. 'They sweat blood filling in all the details on the forms, and I sweat over reading them, wondering what each individual applicant is really like.' It is an acknowledged fact that these forms can *eliminate* just about everyone applying for any type of job.

In theory, the standard form is supposed to show what a man has done and can probably do again in the prospective new job. It does not allow for a man to show how well he did in his last job, and it gives no idea what talents or achievements are needed for the new job. To a person who is determined to climb the ladder of success, backed up by his talents, the idea of applying for another job is to put his feet firmly on the next rung of the ladder, to advance one more step along the road to the top. He knows full well that any further success he has must be achieved by the cold fact that he has done a very fine job for his last employer, and that he is prepared to have a go at doing even better in his new appointment. What he is offering for sale is a commodity that will make a good profit for an employer. In the finality the employer's sole aim is to employ, and keep, personnel who will ensure that the company makes a good and adequate profit.

All the application form will do is to show that the person can do the same work that he has already done. And the executive, or personnel manager, is always assailed by some doubts. 'Maybe the chap has a number of faults if he has had to apply for this job.' Even if the details on the form show that the applicant has had a steady climb from a poor position to one that is much better, the doubts and qualms are still there. 'Why has he only spent an average of two years in any one job? Is he the slick, glibly talking type who gets a new job to avoid being found out in his former situation? Will we become victims if we take him on?' All shrewd employers recognise the fact that if they wish to get rid of a man, and eventually succeed because the man hands in his notice, they will give him a letter of recommendation and heave a sigh of thanksgiving that he has gone, so the new potential employer looks askance at such letters of recommendation. Many of them will only accept such recommendations at their face value if they are from a man they know personally.

Know the application form

The application form is concerned with only what is past. What the applicant is concerned with however, is his future, and so is the company. So why rely upon such a method of finding new employees? Why this concern with what is already obsolete? With job conditions, products and procedures changing so fast today, even the old chestnut 'There's no substitute for experience' has lost most of its significance. Totally new technologies are being spawned overnight, new selling techniques introduced, new accounting methods brought into being, new management skills developing. Computers are taking over old methods, and creating new sophisticated jobs that weren't dreamt of 10 years ago. Change is occurring with bewildering speed, imaginations are being stretched to the limit and thousands of jobs are altered in both small detail and drastic new phasing. As one accountant with 30 years in a large and growing wholesale firm said: 'I've watched my department turned into an electronic, computerised nightmare in the last five years, and found it impossible to keep abreast of the ever-increasing change'. Fortunately for him, he was good at company taxation and set up as a tax consultant. He now has a very flourishing business and makes much more money than he did as a department head in his old firm.

The one thing that doesn't seem to have changed is managerial attitudes to personnel recruitment. Flexibility and a forward-looking modern plan geared to today's conditions should be the basis for finding the person who will adjust to, and keep up with the pace of progress with change — the watchword of today's business world. Engaging staff from an application form can never get beyond the stage of crude trial and error, with management hoping to God they have chosen somebody who will 'fill the bill'. Not someone who will prove to be outstanding, not someone who is the best of all those who applied for the job. No, they acknowledge that that would be too much to expect, so they are satisfied with a choice that can be no better than a pure hit and miss selection. They would almost certainly do as well to close their eyes, take a pin and stick it somewhere on a typed list of applicants' names.

Their concern should be with what a man *could* do, not what was in the past, which is all that the bare impersonal information on an application form can tell them. If managements laid bare their soul, they would admit that they were unable to get more than an absolute minimum of the right people for the jobs they offered through their personnel department, or from agencies. The standard form won't tell them which are the applicants with drive and ambition who know where they are going. These are the people a form will never find. All it will do is to tell them where people have been, with no mention of the vital information — their potential.

You have the drive, the ambition and you know what you want in the future. You know, from your detailed self-analysis and a close study of the market, what the jobs are that will fulfil your immediate ambition. How, therefore, do you circumvent the usual *standard application form*? Even if you have got an interview through a recommendation, you will still be asked to fill a form in where, almost inevitably, your 'Application will receive further consideration, and we'll let you know what we decide!'. So you have reached another dead-end.

Analysing the application form

The standard form starts by asking your name and address, then some personal details such as your age, with your date of birth, marital status, weight and health details. Then it will ask for the title of the position you are seeking. This is quite meaningless because few managements agree on the title and responsibilities of jobs that are offered. After that comes a list of jobs you have held, with the latest job at the top. You are being asked to work backwards, whilst the employer should be looking forward. Some of the details required might prove a positive hindrance to your legitimate claim to have the job offered to you. One or more of the jobs you had might have been a help to your career, whilst others might have had just the opposite effect. You might even have taken jobs for simple expediency, i.e. to keep out of the dole queue. That job might have been quite unsuitable for your talents, but you stayed in it until an opportunity occurred to move on. On the form however, equal emphasis is given to each and all of the jobs you have held and you may appear to have been equally good — or bad — in all of them. According to the form, you are presented to the management as being what the jobs made of you, not what you made of the jobs, or what you expect and are prepared to make of the next.

Look at the typical example below. Like its fellows it needs no imagination, invites cliches, is easy to write and a blatant invitation to a business graveyard where 'application rejected' is the order of the day. Worse than that, *much* worse, is that the boss might quite cynically have decided to give the job to a pal, or the son of a pal, but it is necessary to go through the mechanical application procedure as a means to justify the ends.

Application for the position of Sales Manager, Techprod Corporation

Name and address:	George Smithers, 12 Bruton Street, Anytown
Telephone number:	Anytown 4206
Personal data:	Age 34, married with two children Height, 5 ft 10 in. Weight, 12 stone
Health and details of major illnesses or accidents:	Glasses worn for short-sightedness. Broke leg in motor cycle accident when 18. Influenza followed by pneumonia at 22

Positions previously held:

Jones and Simpson — current position held since 1974
    Sales Administrator — I activate sales campaigns with direct responsibility to the sales manager, arrange exhibitions, sales promotions, direct mail, liaise with

managements of large clients for in-store promotions, analyse salesmen's returns and produce reports for management.

Bloggs & Co. Ltd — Jan 1971 to July 1974
Assistant Sales Manager — was responsible for two major sectors of product promotion, supervised half of the sales force of the company, who were engaged in selling these products. Following recession in this trade, I resigned to join my present company.

Wright and Smith Ltd — June 1965 to Jan 1971
Senior Salesman — I was appointed senior salesman in 1968, following a successful sales career in the company. Was chosen to pioneer some new products. Unable to progress further with this firm, so joined Bloggs and Co.

Education

Bridge Street Primary School, Anytown	Passed 11-plus
Anytown Grammar School	6 'O' levels and 2 'A' levels
Anytown Polytechnic	Passed in Business Methods and Technical Sales Training
	Obtained job with Wright and Smith as salesman at age 22

It could be said that here is the complete business history of George Smithers, and the story of his school career. What more *can* be said? The tragic fact is that the paper now contains the bare bones of what Smithers has done in the past, and says nothing of his plans and hopes for his future, nor of his preparation to make a success of a new and better job. What compounds the tragedy is that thousands of applicants meekly accept that the standard application form is, in their minds, the only method of getting on the shortlist for a job. If their application fails to get them anywhere then it's just hard lines, the luck of the draw. That job has gone for a Burton, so struggle on to the next vacancy and another application form.

Employers and managements ought to realise that the form is of little use in finding the nugget of gold they are looking for in a mass of useless gravel. As I have already mentioned, many do acknowledge the shortcomings of the form, but cannot conceive of anything better, and so the form is accepted with resignation by employers and applicants alike. Any thinking employer looking for people to fill vacancies should be fully aware that such a form gives him no idea of an applicant's potential. He has to guess from reading your past history, crammed into a few words, whether or not you are going to be of value to him in the future. It gives him no idea of the valuable lessons you have learned from your past. All he finishes up with is a number of lists of the number of jobs the applicants have had, and they soon become a series of boring statistics, often leaving the employer with nothing better than pure guesswork to produce the man for his job. So many questions remain unanswered.

How can he estimate, for instance, what value you will be to him because you were in a job that you held — or were stuck with — for five years? It raises many doubts in an employer's mind for all it tells him is who you were employed by, and a very brief resume of what your job was. Perhaps, if you could throw those jobs up — or be fired — it wouldn't be long before you left him, or he had to sack you. There is no room on the form for you to mention that you did a very worthwhile job for your previous employers, and that your growing experience will ensure that you do an even better job for him. What never comes out on the form, and seldom gets mentioned in an interview, is that the employer's greatest concern is hoping he can buy the services of someone whose main purpose in life will be to add to the success and profit of the company. What you did in the past can't achieve that purpose for him, only what you do in the future, and that is something the form never asks.

Success despite the application form

So to the nitty-gritty. How do *you* ensure your success in getting on the shortlist and then securing the job *you* want. Make no mistake about it, if you apply for the job along with many other hopefuls, you will have to go through the normal process of filling in the standard application form. What will give you an advantage over the rest and make the employer sit up and take notice is *your own written resumé*. This will have been prepared very carefully prior to the interview. Fill in the standard form with great care, for this will be scrutinised in detail by the employer and must, in itself, help your case. Having done this to your own satisfaction, attach your own resumé to the form before returning it to the employer.

We have already looked at a standard form filled in by George Smithers, so let's compose a personal resumé for him which should get the special attention he is looking for in his search for a better job.

The strategy he must adopt must be dictated by the sales formula AIDA. As his working life has been spent in the selling game, he will be fully aware of the value of following this formula. He will also realise that the person who will finally decide whether he will get the job in preference to all the other applicants will be the sales director of Techprod Corporation. This chap has very likely clawed his way up to his present position, brushing aside all the opposition in his way, and will be a very hard-bitten individual who has the confidence of the board of directors, which will rely upon him to choose the right man for the job of sales manager. It will be a major success for George to get a favourable reaction from him and to activate a favourable impression before he even meets him.

Bearing all these considerations in mind, and being fully aware of the size of the hurdles in front of him, George must make every step count in his resumé.

Attention What must he commence with to attract the eye? It must be his name and address. It *must* be in the top right-hand corner of the page, so that it will be instantly readable in a file. This is the traditional spot and the one that every person handling that file will look at first. It it's in the middle, or at the left-hand side, or placed several spaces below the top, it will be difficult to see and may be passed over. Still at the top of the page, but on the left-hand side, will go George's age, married status, height, weight and, briefly, his education.

Interest Immediate interest must be gained by stating the objective quite simply and starkly. Then the prospective employer doesn't have to guess what George wants, or be in any doubt that he has confidence in himself in getting there. His interest stimulated, the employer is bound to read the rest of the resume. Having got to this point, George has so constructed his resumé that the employer's growing interest obliges him to take the next step.

Desire Because he is left in no doubt that George has shown enterprise and skill in his presentation of his resume and has put across his strong personality, the employer is quite convinced that he must see this person whose action in presenting this resume marks him as being a cut above his fellows. This leads naturally to the next move planned by George.

Action The employer fixes an interview with George and eagerly anticipates an enjoyable meeting with this 'different' and exceptional applicant. Before he even meets George he has more than half made up his mind that George is the type of man they want for this position. Now the resume itself:

George Smithers
12 Bruton Street, Anytown
Phone Anytown 4206

Age: 34
Married with two children.
Height 5' 10". Weight 12 stone
Educated Anytown Grammar School,

Obtained 6 'O' levels and 2 'A' levels. Obtained first class passes in Business Methods and Technical Sales Training at Anytown Polytechnic.

Objective   SALES MANAGEMENT

Qualifications   Commenced sales career at age 22. Successful sales in difficult areas won promotion to senior salesman in 1968, with special responsibility in pioneering sales of new products. Moved in 1971 having secured position as assistant sales manager. Successfully promoted two major products. Supervised and motivated 50 per cent of the total sales force. In 1974 became sales administrator in present company. I initiate sales campaigns, promotions, direct mail, plan and prepare in-store promotions for large clients. I analyse salesmen's returns and prepare reports to the management. I have technical qualifications and a wide knowledge of technical products. I can successfully present my company's products to the highest executive level of buyers and purchasing officers.

Management   Supervised and motivated sales forces from 1968 to date, commencing with six men and now administering 65, with notable success at each stage and with steadily growing responsibilities. Able to act on own initiative and planning in the areas of sales promotions, exhibitions, campaigns, sales analysis, and producing efficient and succinct reports to the sales director and top management.

Marketing   Market research, field supervision, direct mail and production of in-store promotions for retailers have been amongst my many responsibilities.

I consider that the above qualifications are proof of my fitness to undertake the major job of sales manager of your company. These assets are reinforced by a maturity which ensures that this very big challenge will be tackled with efficiency and an enthusiasm resulting in the success for which you are looking.

This type of resumé is also invaluable in helping to forward your ambitions in the time scale you have set for yourself. When you are ready for another move upwards, there is no need to wait around for the right job to be advertised. Because you will have been planning for this move, you will have compiled a list of firms for which you would like to work. You will know the executive or manager who must be approached. If you have had the time and patience, you will understand the structure of the firm and what is entailed in filling the job you want, so your resumé can be tailor-made to attract the attention and action you want. It is on the cards that you will get around 50 per cent replies and about 30 per cent invitations to an interview. Out of every 20 firms contacted, you should finish up with a choice of two or three jobs.

The invaluable resumé

Whatever your present state — school-leaver, last term in college or university, out of work because of redundancy or any other reason, you can use this effective method of getting a job. It doesn't matter whether you are 16 or 60, boy, girl, man or woman, this type of resumé, which emphasises the positive outlook you have and highlights your talents and ability to be an outstanding asset to the firm you approach, will give you a much greater possibility of success than any other. It is just as effective with public as well as private firms, government bodies and boards; in applying for posts overseas of every type, and in every sphere of work and activity where you want promotion.

Every employer is looking avidly for people who think creatively and your resume, which is the very epitome of creative thinking, will evoke the reaction in many potential employers for which you are looking. 'Now that's the type of chap we've been wanting for a long time', they will say with astonishment and heartfelt thanks. You represent manna from heaven, a potential asset to the company that very rarely occurs.

As I said earlier, see to it that you justify the confidence your new employer has placed in you, for no one falls further than an idol who has been placed on a tall pedestal and then is found to have feet of clay. You are the lonely long-distance runner who has to rely entirely upon himself to reach his goal. You said you could do it, and there'll be no one around if you fall into a muddy ditch on the way. You won the right to be where you are through your own efforts, but that meant telling everyone concerned that you had not only got what it takes to succeed, but that little bit extra that entitled you to preference in the race to get the job that was your goal, so you can't afford to go soft, or relax, on the way. Your talents, backed by dogged persistence that refuses to be deflected from your chosen path, will inevitably make certain that you reach the top of the ladder. In your present firm, or any other.

The programme of success

Your programme should proceed on these lines:

1   State your objective, which is the job you want, emphasising your ability and efficiency in performing well in that position. You are offering the prospective employer a very valuable commodity, and value is what he is looking for. Even though the new job you seek is different in its conception from the one you now hold, your abilities are not affected. Jobs are changing all the time as new methods are introduced. Many even disappear completely when new technology is introduced, but talent will always succeed in getting you where you want to be, so long as you keep you talents sharpened and geared to growing in a fast-changing world. Keep your eyes peeled to see the opportunities that are constantly being created by progress

and change. Don't hesitate to jump in with both feet when the chance presents itself to you. Success goes to the bold, provided the bold are fully prepared to face the challenge.

2   If you are young and ambitious, you may have little or no business experience; *potential* value is what you are offering. Emphasise your youth and ambition, laying stress on those qualities which you have exhibited in your school or college career and which are assets an employer can use to his advantage. Whilst you are selling a 'concept', instead of the actual 'goods' of experience in business, that concept can be very attractive to an employer, if it is presented in the right way.

3   The older person has a very valuable commodity to offer — mature judgement coupled with a deep experience. Don't mention your age in your resumé. If you have got what he wants, an employer isn't interested in your age, only in the value he is going to get if he buys your talents and experience. Many of the top jobs — chairman, managing directors, departmental head on the board of directors — go to men in their 60s. In the Civil Service, government, Parliament, the City, the professions and commerce, it is the rule rather than the exception to award the top job to the person with the greatest experience and maturity, i.e. in his 60s. Many chairmen of large companies are vigorously holding down a full-time job as the top man in their 70s. There is no reason why you shouldn't try for the top if you are 50-plus, even if it means a complete break from a safe job you have been holding down for many years.

Fear of a bleak future is what assails thousands of men when they approach middle-age, and safety is the watchword, often aided and abetted by their wives and families. The world of business and the professions is crying out hungrily for people with maturity and experience, and there are just as many openings available for these people as there are for the younger person. Don't be put off by the adverts offering jobs which say something like: 'Required   Person with Harvard degree in Business Studies to head new department in Personnel Recruitment Company. Must have experience in similar situation. Age not over 30'. Where are they going to find such a paragon who is not yet 30? What they are really saying is that they want someone who won't ask the earth in salary because he is still learning the job. Brash and confident he may be, having got a Harvard degree, but experienced — no. Thousands of advertisements are couched in this form, whilst what the firm really wants is someone with mature experience who can successfully head a department without supervision. This is the person who will give them real value, though it might cost them more in salary. It is time these employers had a rethink. Paying the rate for the job would give them the best value and this is what the mature person could offer.

4   Whilst an employer may give the impression that he knows the exact description of the job he requires filling, and knows in detail what type of person he is looking for, you can bet your sweet life he is never quite sure what he *really* wants. He may be equally certain that he knows what his wife would like for an anniversary present, but if he is offered something more attractive when he is in the mood to spend money, he will buy it. The deal you offer to him must be more attractive than the mental image he has formed of what he thinks he wants. Offer that to him on a plate, and he will snap it up avidly. He has a problem and you have presented him with the solution. He will often go to the point of altering the requirements of the job if your talents, and the value you offer, demand it.

5   Tailor your presentation to the job for which you are applying. Emphasise the facts that support your claim to the job most strongly. What you are asking the employer to do is to imagine you in the job he is offering. Make certain therefore that your talents and experience are set out in such a way that he is left in no doubt that his imagination must be translated into action on his part in offering the job to you. Beware of stretching his imagination to the point where it changes to credulity because you have overplayed your hand in your description of your fitness for the job. Let the plain facts speak for themselves. Tarting them up with over-

emphasis is an excellent way to seriously undermine your case.

6   If you have had several jobs, each contributing to your experience and ability to hold down the new job, try and put these factors into one paragraph. This is going to create a much better impression than breaking down what you did in each job into a list. There is no point in creating in your prospective employer's mind the thought that you have been happy to be in one little job after another. The job he is offering is far bigger than any of them, and he wants a person who has the ability to be master of his size job. Instead, you must make it plain to him that all your experiences have contributed in ever increasing effect to your being the ideal prospect for his job.

7   Finally, and most important. When you have written your resumé, try and assume the role of your prospective employer. He, too, has probably trodden a similar path to yours in getting where he is. A successful man is not likely to forget that he rose to his present eminence through sweat and guts-ache, just like you. If you were in his place, would you buy what you are offering? Think hard and dispassionately about it. If you are satisfied with your own stiff cross-examination and have sold yourself on your own future, you have every likelihood that you will get a satisfied customer in your new employer. The provisions of AIDA will have been fulfilled, and you will have surmounted the next hurdle on the way to your final goal. Whilst the emphasis in this chapter has been on approaching a new employer, the same rules apply exactly in seeking promotion in your present firm. Your task should be less difficult, because you should be able to use your knowledge of your employer to benefit both of you.

Chapter 6

SUCCEEDING AT INTERVIEWS

No matter how well you have prepared your case for getting the job you want, the personal interview with the man who has the power to accept or reject your application is your crucial test. You have reached the point of no return, and you would be a superman not to shrink from an ordeal which is bound to be nerve-wracking. If you have been unemployed for some considerable time, and have already applied unsuccessfully for several jobs, then your confidence in yourself has been undermined.

Take heart though. Your interviewer will probably be as nervous as you, though he is unlikely to show it. His expertise in choosing the right person for the job from the many applicants is being constantly tested, and a few failures will put his own job in jeopardy, so he has to feel his way very carefully. Neither of you have probably seen the other before and you are in the position of two boxers starting a contest without having any idea of each other's strength. An interview is the meeting of two personalities. It should not develop into a clash between you, a defensive-offensive position, but a pleasant exchange of question and answer, and your personal preparation should ensure that the interview from beginning to end is conducted in this fashion.

Many of the methods employed by those who have the hiring power are still the same as they were when an applicant was judged by his physical strength only. 'You look a likely type, you're hired.' If he doesn't give you the job, you're not on his conscience. If he does give the job to you and you fail, he will get the blame. Much easier to let you go and hope that the next in line shows greater promise. It's up to you to show him that you are that person with the *greatest* promise, and leave him no alternative to offering the job to you.

Other interviewers will play tricks on the applicants. If asked why they do it, they will say they want to test the person to see if he reacts well to emergencies, to see if he will 'fit in' with the job and 'meet the demands of the company'. These tricks take all forms and it is wise to be alert to the possibilities of them occurring in your next interview. In some interview rooms, the applicant will find that distractions are applied to take his attention and attempt to loosen his concentration. It may be a window cleaner working briskly directly in view of the applicant. Telephone calls intrude on the interview at crucial moments, people enter to have conversations with the interviewer, breaking concentration. A light will be strategically placed to shine in your eyes to irritate you. Other tricks that have been used are to leave the applicant outside the interview room for longer than is necessary, or even to apparently forget that he is there at all and judge him on how long he takes to knock; to have the door to the room open outwards, making it difficult to enter confidently; to keep a large briefcase on the desk so that it is difficult to see the interviewer when you sit in the chair indicated. Do you stay where you were put and crane your neck, or do you politely ask to move your chair so that you can be more comfortable?

One man interviewed for a top management job entered the room and the managing director said 'Take a chair'; when he did as he was asked, the top of the chair fell off. He was floored mentally for a few seconds and knew he had lost the job. If he'd voiced his thoughts aloud immediately, the reaction to him would have been favourable. Unfortunately, he had displayed hesitation in the face of an unexpected emergency, and killed his chances. The interviewer will apparently lose his own concentration and perhaps drop his eyes on to some papers and fiddle with them; after your voice has hesitated and eventually stopped, he will look up and say 'Sorry about that, you were saying?'.

You must learn to accept these tricks as moves in the game to test you, and to counteract them. Boxers feint to draw their opponent into making a mistake which gives them the opportunity to get in the knock-out uppercut. The interview game uses exactly the same tactics.

Planning a successful interview

The counter-trick you must use is to conduct the interview in the way *you* have planned it. 'How can I do that' you may say, 'when I am the one *being* interviewed, and the employer is the one who should be the person conducting and directing the interview?'. You start with the tremendous advantage that you know the talents you have give you the assurance that you can do the job very well, you have planned the selling job you are going to do for yourself very carefully, you are mentally alert to counter any tricks and you are aware of the best psychological presentation of yourself which will obtain his immediate favourable impression and will continue to maintain his interest to the point where he will offer you the job — or at least put you on the shortlist if that is part of the procedure.

Because an interviewer knows nothing, or very little, about you personally, he is at a disadvantage. This is why so many interviews are conducted in a strained, uncomfortable atmosphere, and why so many employers would sooner have a tooth out than interview people for a job. What invariably makes it worse for him is that most applicants are so vague when interviewed and have no idea how to conduct themselves, or how to present their case, that his eventual choice may be quite unsatisfactory and he can only console himself with the thought that he made the best of a bad job, hoping piously that the person he chose doesn't turn out to be a flop.

Big claims and bluff won't work. Set out to over-awe the interviewer and you'll be out — fast. He doesn't keep his job by being taken in by bluffers, or by the slick and the glib. He *will* recognise and appreciate your self-assurance and confidence backed up by knowing what you want and why you want it. This is the way to put him at his ease and dispel the strained atmosphere. Once this is achieved, you have become friends on a common meeting ground with the same objective in view — making certain that the best choice for the job — yourself — is selected at the end of the day.

What impresses an interviewer? The first moment of contact is through the eye. If he sees someone neatly dressed, hair tidy, shoes clean, making a good entrance without bounce but with confidence, head up and eyes directed to the interviewer, he likes what he sees. Let your face show your confidence, but don't look grim and determined, for that will result in a grimace that will distort your facial muscles and you may look menacing, or just plain comic, and obviously playing a part that doesn't suit you. *Be natural.* If you get the job, the firm has to live with you as you are, not with some act you put on at the interview. You will create and maintain interest which is favourable by being at ease and your own natural self. The package you are selling is *you* and not a box of useless hot air. Even if you reckon you have an ugly face, presenting it naturally to the interviewer always shows its most pleasant aspect. Don't grin or beam all over your face. Practice putting on a small smile if you wish before the interview, but even here there is a danger that the smile can be interpreted as a sign of nervousness, so use such a device sparingly and only if you are sure it helps with your confidence. Close the door behind you gently, but don't turn your back to the interviewer unless there is no other way of closing the door. Walk naturally to the desk, stand about a foot away, and just say, 'Good morning (or afternoon) Mr X', clearly and pleasantly.

Don't say another thing until the interviewer makes the next move. If he is sitting down, he will almost certainly get up, greet you whilst shaking you by the hand, and ask you to sit down in the chair he indicates. This is the next psychological barrier you have to pass. A man's desk is his territory and he doesn't like it being invaded, so don't place the chair so close that you are practically leaning on his desk. On the other hand don't move it so far back that you give the impression of being repelled by him and out of contact. He will be very alert to the way you control your body whilst sitting in the chair during the interview. Are you twiddling your fingers? Taking out your handkerchief several times? Tapping your foot? Swinging your leg? Moving your legs constantly and crossing them alternately? Wiping your face? Holding your shoulders and chin stiff? Smoothing imaginary creases in your jacket? Stroking your face, chin, nose? Sniffing? Clearing your throat often? All, or any of these movements tell the interviewer that you are both nervous and without real confidence in your case, and he may write you off at this point. He will politely continue the interview to the close, but you are as dead as the proverbial dodo.

You are just as dead if you adopt an aggressive attitude. Raising your voice, monopolising the conversation, laying undue emphasis on your qualities, breaking into whatever the interviewer is saying, leaning on his desk. It is amazing that many applicants even allow themselves to get to the point where they bang on the desk to try and get their point over. This is suicide. Familiarity will achieve rejection just as surely. Lounging in the chair, asking if you can smoke, telling jokes, asking personal questions, offering titbits of personal information that have no bearing on the job, reducing the interview to a chat show.

You know that the interview will consist mainly of question and answer. The interviewer will have a set pattern that admits of slight alteration here and there to contend with the differences he senses in the candidate. Each answer is judged on its merits. The interviewer may have a form or pad on which he makes notes, or he may rely upon his shrewd mental assessment of your potential to enable him to make a final judgement. As the interview proceeds so the points are stacked up for or against you. Each interviewee may be allowed a certain time. You may be told how much time can be given at the start of the interview, or you may be told nothing, deliberately, as a test of your ability to keep your side of the interview within a reasonable space of time.

Answer every question simply, with all your facts presented clearly in a totally straightforward manner, emphasising those points which you know should make the best impact. If there is anything in a question you do not understand in any degree, get this cleared before going on to your main answer. Never hesitate to ask for clarification. For all you know, and this does happen, the question may have been asked in that particular way to test whether or not you would ask for clarification, or whether you would try and flannel your way through. You will never lose any points by asking for uncertainties to be cleared up. If the interviewer appears to wander off the main track of the questioning, you have to make a decision to get him back on the rails. Keep it friendly but firm. Again it may be a ploy on his part to distract you and to test your reaction. He may start asking a question which has nothing to do with the job, and the answer could not affect the interview one way or another. Say: 'That is a good question, Sir, but I feel you would really like to hear about . . . (and here you move on to the next telling point in *your* plan for the interview), so may I take that point now?'.

This is a very sensitive and ticklish area, and it would be so easy to upset the interviewer if you became flustered or gave the slightest impression of taking the initiative away from him. He can take no offence if you are gently firm and friendly in your endeavour to get him back on the track. Keep your cool and confident bearing right through and remember that your psychological objective is to get the interviewer on your side right at the beginning and let his liking for you increase right to the end. If he shows any signs of antagonism at all, or cools off in his friendliness at any point, you may as well get up and go, for your chance of the job will have flown through the nearest window. You are dead, full stop. You must maintain a serenity of bearing whilst you are battling away like mad inside and making your personality and achievements felt to no uncertain purpose.

Concluding a successful interview

Make very certain that you have got all your favourite points over before the interview concludes. Anything that is left out may be the one asset that could get you the job, the one thing that would trigger the favourable decision you want. If you have made that favourable impact on the interviewer, he will indicate in some way or other that he has enjoyed interviewing you, and that you stand a chance of either getting the job, or that you are short-listed. It is highly unlikely that he will tell you at that point that you have got the job. The circumstances would have to be very favourable for that to happen. If his final words are: 'Thankyou, and we'll let you know our decision in due course', you are being awarded the final brush-off. Start looking elsewhere immediately. If he gives any indication at all that he liked the way you answered his questions, that he felt friendly towards you, and you will be on the list for final selection, he will tell you so, even if his parting words appear to be non-commital. He will tell you that he would like to see you again, or to hold yourself in readiness for a further interview on the shortlist, or that he would like to think over the points you raised and get in touch.

At the close of the interview don't try and prolong things. If you suddenly remember something you meant to bring up earlier, forget it, it's too late. The interviewer has mentally finished with you and will resent any attempt on your part to start a hare. Thank him cordially for the time he has given you and make a natural exit. Many applicants will ask if they 'stand a chance' of the job, particularly if they have made a number of previous attempts at jobs unsuccessfully and are reaching the point of desperation. It is understandable that they require some sort of reassurance that this time they may be lucky, but such a plea won't do their cause any good. The interviewer has already given you as much information as his routine allows, his mind is already on the next applicant, or the next piece of business ahead of him, and all he wants is to see the door close behind you. If the whole interview has moved along the lines you planned, or has fulfilled your expectations, then be happy with your own behaviour. The last word must always rest with the interviewer. His final decision to award the job to you, or someone else, is out of your control, but if he has displayed a liking for you and your presentation from the beginning to the end of the interview, then you must stand as good a chance as any other applicant, and a much better chance than the majority, who are most unlikely to have prepared themselves to the same degree as yourself.

If you have been informed clearly that a decision will be made within the next 14 days and that you will be notified anyway, you are left with one of two courses to follow. Either you can patiently wait until the decision reaches you in writing, or you can pursue your path to the next job interview. If you have not been given any idea regarding the timing of a decision, then try immediately to arrange your next interview with a new prospective employer. It is by no means unusual for a month or more to elapse before you receive any information, and up to three months before the job commences, so don't let the grass grow under your feet in the interim, but carry on looking energetically. If you finish up being offered more than one job, you are sitting on top of the world, for all your endeavours have been rewarded with complete success; you can choose the best rung on the next step up the ladder.

Using official sources for help

New hope for job-hunters is coming from one or two sources that are seeing the light where training for job interviews is concerned. A few enlightened school careers advisers are running special job interview courses. Even the Department of Education admits that career advice is inadequate in many of the nations 5000-plus secondary and comprehensive schools. They are being pushed by the Association of Teachers in Further and Higher Education to take further adequate action as youth unemployment is becoming a permanent feature of national life. Ron Barrett, Careers Adviser at Henry Thornton School, Clapham Common, London, is running such a special course with marked success. He has convinced the boys that if they try hard enough and follow the advice given in the special interview course, they will find jobs. Once the boys feel they have a chance they find the confidence they need. One of the boys, Michael, said 'I went for an interview, but I couldn't answer the questions properly; now I've had this course, I'll cope. When you know what they are looking for, you can show them what you are worth.' Ron Barrett's enterprise has proved that school-leavers who seem to have all the odds against them can now latch on to a bright hope instead of apathetic acceptance of unemployment. If this is what can be done for black youth in Brixton, then there is still hope for every school-leaver.

The Professional and Executive Recruitment Department (PER) at Manchester University is running a series of courses for adult, middle-level, redundant people of both sexes. The courses are government sponsored and last for eight weeks. During this time the students learn how to project themselves and their talents, as well as being schooled in company law and modern management techniques. The main objective of the course is to prepare the students to be successful at interviews. Of the 272 who have completed the course in the last four years and filled in a follow-up questionnaire, 79 per cent had found jobs, a remarkably high percentage considering that most of the students were middle-aged. This is the most difficult time in life to get a new job after redundancy. Norman Page and Bill Eldridge who direct the courses say that the students feel pummelled and beaten at first, then gradually gain confidence in themselves to the point where they feel truly optimistic about their prospects when they have completed the course. This course is available to the unemployed and they are eligible for financial help from the government. Application should be made to PER at Manchester University.

Similar courses are available in other areas of the country. If you wish to take such a course, get details from careers officers or the job bureaux of the Department of Employment. Do ask if the courses prepare students for being successful at interviews, although with the advice in this book you should have no difficulty in preparing yourself for a successful interview, no matter how awkward the interviewer might be.

The moves which make for a successful interview can be summed up in a few simple sentences:

1   Careful preparation in marshalling your talents which are required for the job.
2   Being ready for any emergency or trick during the interview.
3   Presenting yourself at your best.
4   Being your natural self at the interview.
5   Projecting your personality so that the interviewer likes you.
6   Emphasising those skills which will reward the company best if you get the job.
7   Keeping the interview on a friendly basis to the end.

Chapter 7

PROMOTION

To the success-minded person, the working conditions of today are a godsend. The majority of people in a steady job are cocooned and comforted by automatic regular pay increases, pensions geared to cost-of-living indexes, company benefits such as luncheon vouchers, bonuses, assistance with house purchase, use of a car and expenses, so-called 'productivity' payments, medical benefits, and many other variations of similar themes. It is too easy to fall into the mentally comfortable rut of 'I'm all right, Jack', and to take what is coming, instead of using the abilities and talents they have to rise above the mediocrity of the majority who are willing to accept passively what is handed out to them on a plate. Wages and salaries adjusted to cost of living standards are not increases on merit. Nor are those rises given for length of service. Accent is on retaining the *status quo*.

In many areas, featherbedding is rife and one section of employees is working to keep people in jobs which have become obsolete or produce nothing. What is worse, giving a person an increase in pay because his talents and abilities entitle him to such a rise can lead to problems with the whole workforce, who regard any rise as the prerogative of the whole group with no individual entitled to preference, even though he has manifestly earned it. Therefore the talented person comes to be regarded as a problem by his employers if he puts forward his legitimate claim for an increase in pay. Because this attitude of current working society encourages mediocrity and acceptance of the conditions of employment with the result that extra effort and superior performance is discouraged, the path to success is made very much easier for the talented person to use his initiative and to climb out of the ever increasing mass of people who willingly accept the conditions and who are brainwashed not to 'rock the boat'.

Much of management's time is taken up in 'keeping the peace'; it is to their advantage to discourage one individual who tries to break out rather than to upset the rest of the staff who would demand to know why they could not give everybody the same increase. It would cut no ice to inform them that the rise had been given for 'merit', or 'increased individual productivity', because those are now dirty words. If *one* man gets a rise, there is so much less to share amongst the rest when the next round of pay awards comes up, so that's not on. So the talented, ambitious loner is squeezed between two forces. On the one hand, labour has evolved techniques which seek to get better pay for *all*. This leaves no room for individuals who want to cash-in on their superior achievements, or for individual merit to play a part in negotiations. Management generally tries to keep the peace whilst attempting at the same time to resist demands that go above the fixed maximum limit that can safely be allowed. Everybody knows that agreements are arrived at which are outside the government edict of the day, but the person who has the talents that merit better treatment is ignored totally.

Climbing to the top

The people in management used their individual skills and talents to climb to the top; the labour leader used exactly the same personal achievements to become the top union man; yet both seem to have the same mind and intention to reduce everybody to a conforming mass that can be regimented and moulded more easily. In this kind of society the ambitious individualist represents a problem, the spanner in the works, the thorn that irritates and must be plucked out. This, then, is the opportunity. In any auction sale it is the top-quality stuff that gets the highest bids and attracts the competition of the top dealers. They ignore the mass of mediocre lots in the sale. It is the quality items from which they can make a certain good profit that attract them and for which they are prepared to pay the top market price. Perhaps you don't like being compared with a piece of furniture, but the same criterion applies. You have fine talents for which a willing and eager buyer will pay a high price. It is up to you to devise an attractive package so that eager employers will compete with each other to buy your services at a price that is to your complete satisfaction.

Modern government and union practices are motivated by the spurious and stultifying requirement to negotiate for the working population *en masse*. This movement has now spread right through the complete strata of employment from the newest and lowest-paid worker to management level. Conditions have changed so much during the last decade that many top men in labour and management who fought their way to their present position would now find themselves bogged down in middle-level jobs if they had to begin again, defeated by the very practices they devised themselves.

Let's look at a few of the devices now employed that are calculated to stifle enterprise and initiative and defeat the legitimate claims of talented people to receive wage and salary increases at the point in time when they have earned a rise. Sponsored by the government and now reluctantly backed by the unions, is the 'annual review' whereby salaries and wages are reviewed once a year only, and it is manadatory to award increases at that time and no other. People are told that this ensures a fair deal for everybody at the same time each year, and falls in with government guidelines. Theoretically, your contribution to the efficiency and profits of the firm should then be recognised and rewarded, particularly if your section management have to submit 'personnel assessment reviews' to the board of directors. This latter device is used particularly in some of the largest companies and especially by the multi-national firms. Again, theoretically, you should be given the chance to see and criticise this departmental review before it is submitted to top management, and to demand that anything you don't agree with, on the principle that it is not a fair comment, shall be deleted. I wonder how many insist upon this right? Or how many let it slide because otherwise they might antagonise their immediate boss?

Another device is 'management by exception'. This is based upon the wall graph indicating the heights and troughs of production and sales. It ties in with the annual budget and another chart showing the expected norm of production and sales as forecast in the budget. Thus any deviation from the forecast is immediately noticed and action can be taken. The final graph is the personnel graph, showing what each employee in production and sales is expected to achieve to reach the 'norm'. Theoretically, the departmental manager, or supervisor, should be in a position to spot a person's superior performance as easily as one that is inefficient, and act in accordance, rewarding credit where it is due on the one hand, and dealing severely with the backslider on the other. Unfortunately, for a number of reasons, the deserving seldom get their reward of a wage increase or promotion. The cosy set-up desired by most managers is that of the 'average worker'. This poses no problems. The one who is pulling the team performance down can soon be dealt with and the manager can get him off his back quickly through the normal channels. The talented person who is standing out above his fellows presents the real and difficult problem. He should be recommended for promotion; but if the manager does this another person will be brought in which means an extra burden of paperwork and training, and the manager doesn't relish that. Thus, management by exception can efficiently weed out the inefficient and lazy, but it panders to continued mediocrity and 'average performance' by failing to reward merit.

Finally, there is something management will never admit exists, 'management by inertia'. Here the governing factor is the dictum 'Don't let anything rock the boat and any move must be a bad one'. If there's a problem, cover it up; if anybody wants to dig us out of our cosy nest, sack 'em. Promoting a man will cost far more than the return on the investment because of the cost of training and adjustment to the new job. If we give a rise to one, we must give the same to the lot. If a man is doing a good job, it is safer and easier to leave him where he is than to promote him, because that would entail expense on training. Moreover, perhaps the new man who takes his place may prove to be troublesome, or a flop. Better leave things as they are, we don't want any more problems than we've already got.

By-passing the routine job assessment

Summing up, it seems the prospects for the ambitious person aren't very good in the situations mentioned above. In fact they highlight the escape route for anyone whose progress is blocked by these and similar methods. There are ways of surmounting the barriers in your present situation, and these will be given later, but if you wish to mount the rungs of success in *your* time scale, then there is only one answer. You must change employers and find one who is prepared to reward enterprise and talent with the rate for the job. An inestimable benefit the new job will grant you is the new and greater experience you will get, and need, in your advance to the top. Each change represents a new challenge, a widening horizon, a deeper knowledge of the advances being made in your chosen sphere, and a growing confidence in your ability to tackle and solve the new problems constantly facing you. Staying with one firm can never provide you with that necessary experience, even if you eventually get to the top in your firm. Progress will almost certainly be slower, and your horizons will narrow instead of becoming wider and more challenging.

There is a simple formula which can help tremendously in getting the promotion you are ready for. Note that word 'ready'. This is the key to your success in getting promotion. Take four simple steps:

1   Be absolutely certain you have prepared yourself for

promotion and that you have earned it. Once you are satisfied on this point, you are ready for early promotion.

2. Let your immediate superior be in no doubt that you have earned promotion.
3. Make certain that he knows you know you have earned it.
4. Finally, be quite sure that he knows you know he knows you are ready for promotion.

Complicated? Not a bit. The formula is easy to remember and each step taken helps to build the firm platform from which you will leap on to the next rung up the ladder of success.

No one above you wants problems and least of all do they want yours; the ball is in your court and it is up to you to decide how to play it so that you come out the winner. Keep a written record of what is expected of your job and of your performance in doing the job. Are you fully aware of what you have been doing and how well you have been doing it? If you know you have been performing better than the norm and have been giving no problems to management, there is every likelihood that you are regarded as a sound employee who can safely be put in the 'let well alone' category. So you get neither praise nor condemnation on any part of your work. You are a 'good chap', and they don't want to upset the apple cart by putting any ideas into your head that might cause problems for them. Build up a dossier of your performance, and particularly of those occasions when you exceeded the norm expected of you. Evidence cannot be concrete unless it is documented, so make a note of everything which operates in your favour.

The next step is to let your superior know you have earned a promotion. Not only that; you must endeavour to get him on your side in pushing your claim for promotion. Unless you handle this relationship diplomatically, the result can be disastrous for your hopes. Take him into your confidence. Ask his advice about your plan for promotion, whilst leaving him in no doubt that you are basing your claim on solid achievement. If you show you have above-average talent but don't discuss it with your superior, you become a problem to him. He won't know whether you are saving him work or trying to get his job, and his thoughts will almost certainly incline towards the latter idea. Before you know where you are you will have got yourself an enemy instead of the friend who is an essential part of your plan for promotion. It may be that your documentation of the job will show that he too is worthy of promotion and it won't do your cause any harm to inform him of this.

Keeping vital records

You have got to know you have earned promotion before you ask for it, and you can only be certain of this if you have a written record. There are few managers in the current business world who will go out of their way to tell you that they consider you worthy of a promotion. They may get as far as letting you know you are doing as well as they expected, or that you are keeping to the norm for the job, and hope that you will accept that as a pat on the back and let it go at that. You have been noticed and, who knows, perhaps one day they may give you another bit of praise. When people are mainly concerned with not making mistakes and slipping below the average for the job, instead of carving a bright future for themselves, they will never get out of the rut of mediocrity. Keeping a record of your performance will ensure that you are always looking for the best in yourself. Just tagging along with the rest, on their level, just achieving the norm for the day, won't give you anything to record of any significance. If you find yourself slipping into this way of working, pull yourself up and start making a contribution to your record again. As you are aiming for the top, you must be your own sternest critic to ensure that you will not fall behind in keeping up to the standard you have set for yourself.

Don't make the mistake in your planning of aiming too low when you go for promotion. Far too many people have accepted an alleged promotion which has been little more than a sideways move, mollifying themselves with the thought that they have achieved recognition for the good work they have done. Receiving the pat on the back from the management has given them more satisfaction than getting a true promotion worthy of their achievements. On the other hand the company will not be interested in awarding promotion to the position you know you can fill unless they have very good evidence that such a promotion represents a profit for the company. Let us say that you base your claim for promotion on a plan that will save the company around £6000 per annum because you can bring more efficiency to the new job. They are hardly likely to promote you to that level if it means they have to increase your salary by £3-4000. You won't have contributed a penny extra to profit. The savings will have to be around £20,000 to justify such a promotion. Your plan therefore will have to include a copper-bottomed base of company profit before the management will listen to your claim for the job you want.

Even if you kept your immediate manager in the picture with your plan for promotion and have got his apparent support, it is possible that you have become a very valuable asset to him and that he is relying more and more on your abilities and performance in keeping his department working efficiently and smoothly. Any promotion you got therefore would mean losing your services and replacing them with an unknown quantity. With the best will in the world, and whilst outwardly wanting to help you, he will probably do his best to delay your move. If you have evidence that this is happening, and your time scale is being jeopardised, then you are presented with a big obstacle that has to be overcome. You may be faced with the company system that insists on the lines of command being sacrosanct. In other words, any move towards promotion must be through your immediate manager and his personal recommendation. There are two alternatives in this situation. You can either apply for a job in another firm, or you can by-pass your manager. You have fully established the fact that he knows you know he knows of your plan to get promotion, but he won't write the actual recommendation for an interview with the manager or director who can award such a promotion. Having an unpleasant open confrontation with your immediate manager will only result in bad feeling and possibly a strong complaint being registered with higher management. Applying steadily increasing persuasive pressure will achieve your ends eventually, but may still leave a residue of bad feeling, and you may acquire the tag of being a complainer from your manager and a creeper from your fellows. Your self-confidence may be labelled as arrogance and egotism.

Surmounting promotion obstacles

Request a private interview with the key executive who would be handling the question of your promotion if it had been recommended through the standard channels. Such a request can be either written or made on the telephone. Your genuine reason for such an interview is that you have certain ideas and plans that would be of particular interest to him. At the interview give him your written record and report to read. After reading it, he may hand it back to you saying, 'What do you want me to do about this?'. Tell him what you really want is his advice. You have kept your own manager up-to-date with your plans and you like working in the company. You feel that you have contributed significantly to the efficiency of the department, but you seem to have reached a dead-end. Perhaps the only thing to do is to look around for another job. What would he advise you to do? He is relieved that you are asking his advice and not making a demand of any kind, so he is not being committed. On the other hand, you have handed him a challenge to his position. If he is even half-convinced that you have a valid case for consideration for promotion, then he will take steps to see that the company does not run the risk of losing your valuable services. The ball is in his court now to circumvent the system to benefit you, whilst allowing your own manager to make the official move of recommendation. The *status quo* is thus retained and the company system maintained without loss of face to any individual.

The success you have achieved in gaining your ends has meant using company politics, albeit you may never have realised you were playing politics. From this moment on in the new position you have won, company politics is the name of the game. You have advanced to a position with a title, and you are the new head of a team working under your direction. The new responsibilities you have gained have enhanced your prestige and power in the company. The material gains may be significant with accompanying additional benefits — company car, more holidays, better pension, profit-sharing, etc. — and almost certainly played a big part in shaping your plans for promotion. You have, however, now entered a different working world with entirely new rules. Previously you had two simple main concerns — how well you did your job, and what the boss thought of your work. Now many other people are your immediate concern. New relationships alter your approach to the new position. Your plan of campaign encompasses a much wider field and your responsibilities are both wider and heavier. Not only must you ensure that you and those under you do a good job of work, better and more efficiently than it has ever been done before, but you must be concerned about what a whole stratum of people think about you, what you think about them, and how to control the constantly changing interaction between them.

Your subordinates will look at you and regard you with a very critical eye until you are either OK or a failure, in their judgement. Your superiors will be monitoring your performance constantly, and this means you in particular and your department in general. The other managers on your level, and on the next level above, will watch you very warily. Any new entrant into their sphere of influence represents a potential danger and they will be ready to pounce on any shortcomings on your part in order to safeguard themselves. It is not unknown for an executive to mount a campaign against a newcomer to his level whom he regards as a potential threat to his place in the pecking order of the company. When you are concerned directly with people and play a part in their direction, you enter politics, a game in which there are no neutrals, only those who are smart and those who are outsiders. If you are to continue to climb the ladder to the top, you must be as smart as those you meet on the way, and try to keep ahead of the game all the time.

The one big advantage you should have when you enter this political jungle for the first time is that you know your own capabilities to the nth degree; the confidence resulting from that knowledge will give you the power to play a winning game. Success builds on itself. As you progress towards your goal, your confidence increases at the same pace as your responsibilities. At some stage you will pause to take a breather and say to yourself, 'I never thought I would be capable of holding down a position of such responsibility when I began in this game', but sober reflection shows that as you have climbed to each peak, your horizons have widened and your capabilities have increased. It is always a less daunting prospect contemplating the next step up the mountain even though the path may be more difficult. The higher you go, so your experience grows in handling the bigger responsibilities, and you have more people below you to help you along the way. Beware of reaching the same stage as thousands of executives for whom the growing responsibility and increasing pressures become appalling burdens, and they slacken off and falter when the going should be at its best. If you have maintained your personal assessment record, you will avoid that pitfall, for you will know exactly when you are ready, willing and able to take the next step forward. If you have chosen your team well, instead of relying on the old worn-out test and recommendation system, then you have loyal colleagues and subordinates who are contributing positively to your plan for their own good as well as yours.

Let me emphasise once again that continuous success can only come from a constant study and understanding of your talents and achievements in relation to the goal for which you are striving. It is a constantly growing situation in which your increasingly valuable experiences enrich your business ability, acumen and your whole personality. Opportunities exist at all stages of the business game, but the initiative to seize those opportunities lies squarely on your own shoulders. Never expect that opportunity will come looking for you, or that success will be handed to you on a plate. Not in the current business world. You must put your entire trust in your own self-reliance; in the power of your own talents and achievements.

Chapter 8

STAYING AHEAD IN A CHANGING WORLD

Most people will say that their aim is a good job that will give them security. That is their formula for achieving success. I've got news for them. In the fast-changing world of today, their 'secure' job may be swept away and they could be redundant. Whole industries can wither overnight, and new processes can make sectors of manufacturing obsolete. Even those jobs that were regarded as the safest, i.e. in government service, or in nationalised industries, are no longer secure. Mergers, takeovers, rationalisation, moves of firms to new locations, all lead to jobs that have been regarded as secure for decades being swept away. Even the basic industries on which the prosperity of the country has been built become the victims of the fast-changing times. Shipbuilding, fishing, steel, the wool and cotton industries, cars, building and other basic manufactures are suffering from major troubles which could not have been envisaged a few years ago. People whose jobs were as secure as the Bank of England, or so they thought, in industries that had supplied security to their fathers and grandfathers before them, find themselves redundant overnight after spending their whole working life in their 'secure' job. New machines and technologies replace the old, needing less people to operate them. No one is safe. The business pages of the newspapers are continually reporting cases of men in top management losing their jobs. Chairmen and managing directors of public companies are sacked and tens of thousands of people in middle management are swept away into the dustbin of redundancy.

Attracting much less publicity than the traumatic events listed above is the undoubted fact that the new technologies, new machines, new managements, and the new areas of industry are crying out for personnel who have kept up with the times, who have geared themselves to face up to the challenge of change and become trained in the new methods which offer a rewarding and exciting future. Those men in electrical engineering who saw the new electronic age dawning and who took the decision to become trained in the new technologies, are now leaders in the industries which electronics spawned and which relentlessly disposed of the old mechanical processes. From calculators to computers, control systems to aerospace, the golden opportunities presented themselves in a deluge that hasn't diminished, and those who took advantage of converting their talents into becoming trained operatives and managers are now reaping the benefits of their foresight. Many an office machine mechanic, trained on hand-operated typewriters, who took the trouble to take training on the first electric typewriters and then the electronic calculator and copier, is now in a flourishing business of his own, servicing and maintaining these electronic marvels. The same goes for the men who serviced the old mechanical data processing machines and moved into computers by taking a series of training sessions. Most of this essential training was offered on a plate to mechanics by the manufacturers of the new machines, at a very cheap rate, for every new machine they sold had to be serviced by somebody so it was essential that the manufacturers offer this training to ensure that they could, in turn, offer the equally essential back-up service to their clients.

Cashing in on change

The man who preferred to stay in his old apparently safe job of servicing the mechanical machines that had provided him with a living for all his working life now finds himself either redundant, or relegated to the drudgery of the service workshop, keeping the fast-dwindling numbers of old machines in working trim for small users, or for the second-hand market. Thousands of mechanics were known to have said that these new machines were 'gimmicks' and they would never replace the old reliable machines that had been doing a good job for decades, and which had only had small improvements in all of that time, leaving the basic technology comfortably unchanged. This is the man who is being left behind and whose job will disappear for ever. The young and eager person who is trained in the new methods and who is constantly keeping himself familiar with the modifications and improvements being continually brought out is the technocrat of today who will make a success of his talents and create the new jobs spawned by the ever-changing modern world. Life from the beginning of man's existence on this planet has been governed by the immutable law of the survival of the fittest. It is the man who keeps himself mentally fit to cope with and master the demands of today's business world who will be the successful survivor.

In a survey conducted some time ago, it was revealed that over 75 per cent of working people are in jobs that do not use their best abilities, and therefore do not provide the satisfaction associated with success. Such an appalling revelation triggered off no concerted action on the part of any official body and, for that matter, no action was taken by anybody to see if such a situation could be rectified. This state of affairs has gone on for so long, probably for centuries even, that it is taken totally for granted as a fact of working life that must be accepted because there is little anyone can do about it. What this means is that 75 per cent of working people are satisfied to just 'tick over' in their jobs, whilst their best abilities atrophy. They are endeavouring all the time to maintain a routine mediocre performance that will just keep them on the payroll. Is there any wonder that the person who sets out to use his best talents and achievements to progress up the ladder of success finds his way made easy by the inertia of the majority? Can you imagine the prosperity that would accrue to all if the hidden, dormant talents of the 75 per cent majority of working people were harnessed and working flat-out for the economy? The increase in productivity would be immeasurable, as would the increased well-being and happiness of the whole population.

Achieving success with happiness

True success has only one criterion — the achievement of real happiness. Success cannot be measured solely by material things it showers on the recipient. Without happiness, there can be no true success. Many millionaires could not describe themselves as being happy people. They occupy their time in chasing an ephemeral happiness that never truly materialises. Their odd activities keep gossip columnists busily engaged whilst they flit from one 'in-place' to another in a furious competition to keep themselves in the news. Happy? Not even remotely. These are the people who have never had the satisfaction of using their undoubted talents in getting where they are, or whose minimal use of their talents has been seized upon by agents and speculators to project them like a rocket into a material prosperity for which they were totally unprepared and which usually ends up destroying them. Success can only be measured by the criteria you set for yourself. Material success may not enter into your search for happiness. Your success may lie in rendering exceptional service to others worse off than yourself, using all your talents in this direction. Using skills to devise new aids to help the handicapped may not put an extra penny in your pocket, but such a success, and the happiness that goes along with it, cannot be given a price. Playing for your country in an amateur sport, mastering the hazards of a difficult mountain or flying a small plane for the first time, are just a few examples of success with true happiness.

Never regard any successes you achieve as being the sum of your potentiality. No one ever reaches the point where they are using *all* their talents to the limit. If they were they could justifiably be called the perfect human being, and such a marvel has not yet been born, nor is ever likely to be. What you must realise is that you have within you an enormous reservoir of potential success that will remain virtually untapped, and this applies to everyone. You will never plumb the depths of your total potentiality. We deeply admire and marvel at the success of severely handicapped people in not only coming to terms with life, but surmounting seemingly impossible difficulties. As far as lies in their power, they have achieved success with happiness. If the rest of us would only set out to use the powers that we have to the same extent as handicapped people, then we would scale heights we never dreamt of reaching before.

You are on your way if you awake each morning filled with anticipation of what achievements you can perform during the day, happy that if you strive to do your best you can expect the reward of your endeavours. If you ever find yourself waking with the thought 'Oh, God, another day to get through', or with any sense of resignation whatsoever, then pull yourself up very sharply and re-appraise your situation. Start digging into that well of potentiality which you possess. Begin another analysis of your talents and achievements. This exercise may well reveal new slants on your abilities which you never realised were there and will get you back on the track where you are once again using your best potentialities.

Everyone around you will benefit if you are doing your best and they will contribute towards your future successes. This service to others will lead much more quickly to your success in getting ahead than by ruthlessly climbing over others.

Competition there must be to bring out the best in you, to provide the spur that keeps you on your toes. A good measure of how choice a job is for which you are applying is the mettle and worth of the competition. If there is no competition, or it is poor, then the job is suspect and you should look at it very carefully before applying. Keen rivalry is bound to bring out your best qualities in business just as much as it does in sport. No sportsman or team worthy of the name flourishes unless they are striving to beat rivals of their own, or better, calibre. They know this is the only way to improve their own performance. Training will help, but it is only in the open field of competition that new heights can be reached. Be pleased for yourself if the competition is fierce for this is what is needed to give you the added strength to come out top. Without such rivalry you will never know just how good you can be. If you lose out now and again and someone pips you at the winning post, sit down and analyse the reason for your defeat and profit from the lesson. Never worry about your defeat for worry is self-defeating anyway. No one yet has won all the things they want at the first go, so you are in good company. If you know you have done your best, then perseverance will win the next round for you.

Realising your potential

Knowing what is best in yourself and realising your potentials will promote you to the position where you are in charge of other people. We have already seen that 75 per cent of working people are performing well below their capacity and regard each day as something to be got through so that they can enjoy their leisure. The man who is the best and most successful employer, or manager, is the one with the best employees who are happy to do their utmost in the interests of the job, themselves and their employer. It is up to you to make a habit of recognising what is best in those under you. Search out and utilise their talents.

Remember Robin Rippin, featured in Chapter 2. He was thrown out of his job in a garage because he was 'cheeky' and 'useless'. Then his boss in the agricultural machine repair shop refused to listen to his good ideas, so he left and set up on his own. If either of these two worthy gentlemen had sat down and thought about the potential value of Robin to them, they could have founded an unbeatable team, each contributing their best talents towards what would have become a very successful firm. As it was they both ended up contributing nothing to their own firms, whilst their erstwhile 'useless' employee was leaving them standing in the race to success. I wonder how many employers have said ruefully to themselves, 'Oh, if I had only known how good that chap could be', after someone has left them and become successful in another position.

Finding and utilising other peoples' talents and potentiality, discovering their best qualities, will be rendering the best service possible to them and to yourself. This is where your strength and the strength of your team will stand head and shoulders over any competition, ensuring success for all. Some of the more enlightened boards of directors are slowly realising this fact, and encouraging managers to find and develop the hidden talents of their people. Putting this business philosophy into practice has far greater practical results than relying on sterotyped assessment forms produced at the end of each business year which usually finish up in some dusty filing cabinet.

Some day, instead of 'working for a living', people's abilities will be recognised and their real talents harnessed by management for the benefit of all. Until that time arrives, realise quite firmly that you are on your own. You are in charge of your own abilities, and only you can chart the path of your success which those abilities can achieve. Be self-sufficient and secure in knowing your capabilities, regardless of any outside influence which seeks to deflect you from the path you have chosen. Be of service to others who will be working with you. Recognise and develop their talents alongside your own, and nothing in this world will stop your progress to the goal for which you are aiming — success with happiness.

All the reasons listed earlier in this chapter for the fast-changing world, disposing of the old ideas of job security, emphasise the fact of 'ability security'. Obsolescence, new technologies, new processes, greater emphasis on automation, mergers, takeovers, scientific discoveries, are the symptoms of progress and opportunity. Changes induced by these factors can be totally traumatic to those who have always buoyed themselves up with the anodyne, 'Oh, my job is safe'.

When their job disappears, they find themselves in a disastrous position because they have made no preparation for such a situation, even though there might have been indications that change was coming. On the other hand, the man who has kept up with the times and constantly geared himself to the new processes and methods is the man who welcomes the change, for it represents a new challenge and opportunity to exercise his talents. His ability will ensure his growing security. Each change will be used adroitly to further his designs and project him further up the ladder of success. Changes will be at an even faster rate as computer-based technologies escalate. It is estimated that new types of jobs are being created at a rate of over two per cent per annum, and old ones correspondingly disappear. In 10 years' time 1 in 5 people will be employed in jobs that don't even exist at present!

On the other side of the coin, it is equally true that 3 out of 10 people are now being trained for careers that will be as dead as a dodo in 10 years' time. Don't let that dismay you though. The talents and achievements you are assiduously cultivating will assure you of a slice of the new action when it comes along. It's not the label on the job that matters, but the calibre of the person who chooses it. Will you be far-sighted enough to prepare yourself for the new challenges that change brings and grab the opportunities that will be on offer, or will you attach yourself to the label your present job gives you and hang on to it no matter what? Believe me, the world is an oyster, full of rich pearls for the taking, for the person who has learnt to use his abilities for his own progress and for those who work with him. He is always welcoming the future and the wonderful world of opportunity, instead of bewailing the fact that 'things aren't what they were in my father's day'. Your father could look 10, or even 20, years ahead to the time when steady application to his job could reward him with the management of the department in which he had always been an employee. He concerned himself with one sole aim, the narrow path to the head of a certain department. He had firmly attached himself to a label and refused to be parted from it. In those days it would have been cataclysmic if the department itself disappeared at the end of 10 or 20 years. It was entirely normal to enter a firm at 16 years of age and work up to departmental manager at 50 or even 55, and to retire gracefully at 65 with the accolade of a gold watch from the boss.

Keeping on top in a changing world

You are kidding yourself if you think this state of affairs still applies, so don't saddle yourself with the label of a job. The name of the game now is *change*, with its new philosophies, new attitudes, new products, new careers. The still, unruffled surface of the past has become the whirlpool of the present. Those who survive and succeed are the people who rely upon themselves and know they have a fine package to offer to the new brand of employers who are crying out for the person with talents geared to modern conditions and the ability to cope with and overcome the problems spawned by technologies that are reaching into the unknown.

The future is just as exciting for women as for men. The increase in leisure provides more and more openings in areas like national parks, conservation, travel in all its forms — air hostesses, couriers, travel agents, holiday camp and villa managers, etc. World-wide politics and diplomacy provide good jobs for girls in secretarial positions, as translators, couriers, and much more. The agencies of the United Nations, the Common Market, diplomatic missions, government-sponsored business trade fairs and exhibitions all need women in dozens of different, exciting and interesting jobs that have world-wide travel to offer as a bonus. The world of fashion has become truly international and models and cosmeticians are in strong demand as well as women in all departments of management.

Demolish the walls of your complacency and look critically at yourself with a view to discovering those talents you had forgotten, or discarded, because they never appeared to be of any cash value. Determine to wake yourself up — nobody else will do it for you — and seek the bright new world that is desperate for your talents; the community service that can use your abilities to improve conditions for the sick,

old, handicapped; the business sector which will provide
the training for the job for which your talents are ideally
suited. Revive the desire to start a business for yourself.
Almost every positive attribute you may have will provide
a sound base for starting your own business. Rediscover
and dust off the experiences and achievements in all you
have done in your life to this point. Build on them in your
preparation for the true fulfilment of your life. The best job
still lies ahead, so forget the past and get cracking into the
bright new future.

Rising above the average

How do you know you are performing at your best? What
measurement is there to tell you that you are using your
talents to the maximum? Look around you at the people
with whom you are working. Management judges the performance of the business and its employees on a known
factor, 'average performance'. This is a certain quality that
can be charted on a graph, and everyone in that business
is fully aware of the requirements necessary to reach and
maintain that 'average performance'. It does not matter
in what sphere you are operating, the same criteria applies
if you are in employment of any kind, and in every level
from cleaner to chairman. It is given many labels, such as
'measured work norms' and many others peculiar to the
particular trade or manufacture. It may not be given a label
in so many words in the professions, or offices, but it is
there none the less and is known and recognised as a factor
in employment. All you have to do is to look critically at
your own performance. Do you qualify as an 'average
performer'? Is your position on the graph the same as the
majority? If so, then take hold of yourself and determine
to give free reign to your talents and achievements instead
of restricting them. Let them hoist you above the mass
mediocrity. Don't set your course a notch above the
average. Use your abilities to reach for the top. Never be
content with being average or just a little better than average.
Knowing your abilities and how much better they are than

the average is the spur needed for using them to the limit to achieve the goal you have set for yourself. In making a habit of success, you establish a habit that becomes incurable.

In Chapter 2 some of the talents that can be used to get the job you want were mentioned. Here is a checklist of the personal attributes that can be harnessed to assist you in the pursuit of your goal. Make a note of those which you feel have contributed in some way or other to your achievements, and any which have given you some personal satisfaction when you have employed them in any way. It does not matter if using them brought you no personal gain. If you liked using them, then put them on your list. Some you may not have thought about, or used, for many years, so spend some time in close study and dig back into your memory to rediscover what you liked doing when you were a child or at school. Any that ring a bell put on your list.

When you are quite sure you have made a complete list, you may be surprised to find that a dozen or more items appear on your paper. Whatever you do, don't have second thoughts, or any doubts, and start crossing some off. Something positive prompted you to put all those items down, so they all start level on the next part of the exercise.

Harnessing your talents

Your next task is to choose those attributes which appear to you to be the most important. Which did you like using most? Which gave you the greatest satisfaction? Which were you most reluctant to give up when moving from childhood into the adult state? Which do you know in your heart are those which will help you most in pursuit of your personal success? Start by placing one X against those you find most attractive. This might have reduced the number to between 5 and 8. Consider these in greater depth, and put another X against those which are outstanding in your mind. Now you are down to 2, 3, or 4.

Don't pursue the exercise to the nth degree in order to try and find out which comes out top. You are not constructing a league table and none of us can achieve real success on the strength of one principal asset only. You are looking for three or four powerful allies which will always be at hand to make failure impossible; attributes that will help and sustain you in your climb up the ladder of success, to the goal you have chosen. Cultivate these talents to increase their power and efficiency in the same way that a top athlete cultivates his bodily strength in order to break records. The mind can respond to training and concentration to a far greater degree than the body, and you don't have to put a ceiling on your ambitions. If pushed to the limit, the body will break under the strain, but the trained mind can achieve the seemingly impossible and still be eager to reach further, fuelled by your concentration on the things you like doing best. Don't forget the second choices, those which received only one X. They can be called on to help in the campaign when required. So to the checklist:

Do you like	ANALYSING
Are you	ARTISTIC
Do you like constructing	BUDGETS
Can you	COORDINATE
Are you in any way	CREATIVE
Do you like	DESIGNING
In any project do you get down to	DETAILS
In your work or play do you use	DRIVE
Are you	ECONOMICAL
Do you enjoy working with	FIGURES
Have you got	FORESIGHT
Do you like dealing with	HUMAN RELATIONS
Are you full of	IDEAS
Can you exercise your	IMAGINATION
Are you an	INDIVIDUALIST
Can you exercise your	INITIATIVE
Are you	INVENTIVE
Do you like being the	LEADER
Can you sympathetically	LISTEN
Does it appeal to you to be a	MANAGER
Does your mind lean towards being	MECHANICAL
Do you like dealing with	MONEY

Do you like taking part in	NEGOTIATIONS
Are you a keen	OBSERVER
Do you like being an	ORGANISER
Are you keen on the	OUTDOORS
Do you like to be an	OWNER
Do you like being with	PEOPLE
Are you	PERCEPTIVE
Can you	PERSEVERE
Do you like controlling	PERSONNEL
Are you	PERSUASIVE
Do you like being a	PLANNER
Can you take part in	POLICY-MAKING
Do you like	POLITICS
Are you	PRACTICAL
Do you like	PROBLEM-SOLVING
Do you like being involved with	PRODUCTION
Do you like making	PROGRAMMES
Do you like	RESEARCH
Do you find satisfaction in	SELLING
Do you like doing people a	SERVICE
Have you a flair for	SHOWMANSHIP
Can you express yourself in	SPEAKING
Do you like working with	SYSTEMS
Would it appeal to you to be in	TRAINING
Are you interested in	TRAVEL
Are you fascinated by	WORDS
Do you find fulfilment in	WRITING

Any combination of three or more of these talents fulfils the requirements of the job that appeals to you and which you would like to get, as the examples in Chapter 3 point out. Let's look at a typical selection of good jobs offered in one day's edition of the Daily Telegraph and see which talents are needed from the above checklist:

Management of large regional retail stores Analysing – Budgets – Details – Figures – Human Relations – Ideas – Initiative – Leader – Manager – Organiser – People – Personnel – Problem-solving – Selling – Service – Speaking

— Systems — Training — Eighteen in all. If your three best achievements are in the field of Human Relations, Organisation and Selling, then you have an excellent base for projection into a job such as the above. All the other requirements are related to these three, or can be cultivated quickly. If you are already in a job in a multiple store, these talents can enhance your chances of getting a job in retail management.

Personnel manager   Coordinate — Drive — Foresight — Human Relations — Leader — Listen — Manager — Negotiations — Observer — People — Personnel — Persuasive — Planner — Problem-solving — Speaking — Training — Words — Writing — Eighteen again. Your three best talents could be Human Relations, Leader, Problem-solving.

Market research and development   Analysing — Budgets — Coordinate — Details — Ideas — Imagination — People — Planner — Practical — Research — Showmanship — Speaking — Writing — Thirteen talents. Your three best could be Ideas, People and Research.

Operational research officer (Gas Corporation)   Analysing — Coordinate — Creative — Details — Ideas — Initiative — Organiser — People — Problem-solving — Research — Systems — Eleven in this case. Suggested three best: People, Research, Systems.

Senior salesman   Creative — Details — Drive — Human Relations — Imagination — Individualist — Negotiations — People — Persuasive — Selling — Showmanship — Speaking — Travel — Twelve items. Three best: People, Persuasive, Selling.

Whilst it is advisable to already be in a job in those fields mentioned above, as experience can assist, there are dozens of good jobs available which can employ your talents if you will only relate those talents to the job. Chapter 3 tells you how to create your opportunity and how to use the AIDA formula to secure the job. A good job in selling, for instance, can be yours if you have three or more of the talents listed above for the job of senior salesman. It doesn't matter what job you have now, or if you are out of work; you can build you own case for securing the job you want in selling. Find your talents, relate them to the job you would like, write your programme and your resulting selling campaign is bound to result in success. And this same formula applies to every sphere of employment. Use your talents and achievements to become the master of your own fate.

The French song, *My Way*, made popular in the English version by Frank Sinatra, sums it all up very well:

> Regrets I've had a few, but then again too few to mention.
> I did what I had to do and saw it through without exception.
> I planned each charted course, each careful step along the highway,
> And more, much more than this, I did it my way.
> For what is a man, what has he got if not himself,
> Then he has to say the things he truly feels,
> And not the words of one who kneels.
> The record shows I took the blows, and did it my way.

Chapter 9

STARTING YOUR OWN BUSINESS

David John Brown made himself a multi-millionaire in only four years, despite the slump in world trade. How? By having the confidence to back his own talents and achievements. In his own words, 'By having confidence in one idea, knowing from experience that if *I* made it, *I* could sell it, and being determined to do it for myself and not for somebody else'. The idea was to make a six-wheel heavy-duty dumper truck for construction work in rough territory. He had designed earth-moving machines for a firm in Gloucester, and at 48 he decided that his idea for a new type of machine had to see the light of day. So, with the help of his son, David, he threw up his good job, sold his home in the Cotswolds, borrowed some money privately, and found that if he took a factory in the development area of Peterlee in Durham, the Department of Industry would lend him £80,000 more to create employment there. He did the designing and drawing, whilst his son built the office partitions and storage cupboards. Whilst it took 18 months before a prototype machine was ready for trying out, his drawings had secured some orders, and he had set up an embryo dealer distributorship system. From his experience in the field he knew what the user really wanted, whilst with his very big competitors there was a chasm between what they made and what the potential customer needed. His new machines soon proved their worth in tough conditions in the Yorkshire Dales and even tougher, rougher country in the Congo.

When he moved to Peterlee, he could not afford to buy a house and moved into a council house on an estate. Because his enterprise proved an outstanding success from the start, backed by his overwhelming confidence in his talents and determination to succeed, he was parking a Rolls Royce and a Mercedes outside the council house and flying a company aircraft from Teesside airport less than two years after starting up for himself.

Now his turnover is around £15 million per annum with 97 per cent being exported. He has provided good jobs for 400 people and is confident that his turnover will be £100 million in seven years, with a workforce in the thousands. What about any slump that might occur in that time? David says, 'World trade is not an entity that is going to pick up of its own accord. It will only pick up if a lot of people like me *make* it pick up.' Now he has got around to moving into a new house and is starting on his development scheme, with his eyes on a 200-ton payload vehicle that will cost each customer around £500,000, and on vehicles which an army can use in any kind of terrain, whether it's the Arabian desert, swamps, or rough mountain country. His final words should be a lesson to everyone, and particularly to those who try to control our destinies: 'The best man to keep in touch with the customer is the boss himself. That is impossible for firms that get too big, for they have to send out salesmen who usually know little about engineering. *It's the same with labour relations. They can only be good if the boss knows all his men. British industry would be far healthier if bosses took more risks. Nobody gets far if they rivet their eyes on security.*' It's a pity these words cannot be riveted into the minds of the powers that be, so that men like David Brown could be given every encouragement.

Pursuing a good idea

If you have a good idea, cultivate the confidence, determination and single-mindedness of David Brown, then follow in his footsteps. Ignore the prophets of doom who tell you 'It can't be done, the risks are too big, you'll be bankrupt in a year, so stick to your old, safe job'.

There is no field of activity which cannot provide an opportunity to the man who has a talent. I remember giving a lift to a fellow salesman in my car some years ago. He was obviously prosperous, and explained that his car had developed a fault and was in a local garage being repaired. Instead of standing around waiting for the repair to be finished, he determined to hitch a lift to his next call. We got into conversation, and I asked him what he was selling as he was obviously making a pretty good living. 'I make and sell dartflights', he said. 'Just dartflights?' I asked, 'Because if that's all you sell, how do you manage to do so well for yourself?'. 'It's because I've made a study of them, and finally came up with something that's now acknowledged to be the best dartflight on the market. I've concentrated all my efforts on perfecting these flights, and now I know I'm making and selling the best. I have no difficulty in selling all I can turn out at a pretty good profit. An absorbing hobby now gives me prosperity.'

If that fellow could make a success of making and selling something as unlikely as dartflights, the field of opportunity must be as wide open as the far horizons. Making something, being of service. There are many thousands of different ways of carving out a success for yourself. The only things you have to ask of yourself are 'Have I the talent?', 'Have I the confidence and determination?' and 'How do I get started?'.

Profiting from leisure

People who have enjoyed doing something in their leisure time with no thought of making a living from it have discovered that here was a talent that could bring them success with fun. Young people who can perform reasonably well on a musical instrument find they can command quite high rates per hour by playing to the public. Travelling discotheques, musicians performing in small groups playing for dances and parties, or individually, can command sums of £25 and upwards for three hours' playing in the evening.

Men and women who liked playing the electronic organ have set up organ shops, started magazines for organ lovers, opened up teaching centres. Golf afficionados have gone professional, run golf shops, sold golf equipment. Mountain climbers, walkers, cyclists, motor cyclists, car drivers, lovers of the outdoors, footballers, hang gliders, and any number of people with a sporting hobby have carved out a successful business for themselves opening shops to sell the gear connected with the sport, or gone into manufacturing when they have had ideas for better equipment, or set up as agents for home and continental manufacturers. You name the hobby, or the talent, and a successful business can be built on it. I bet the chap who first mooted his idea of setting up a business making and selling dartflights was laughed to scorn by his relations and friends, but he knew he had the talent, so he ignored the doubting Thomases and just did it his way. This mental attitude, coupled with his undoubted talent, ensured his success from the word go.

Dogged determination and supreme confidence in his own abilities have made young Eddie Kidd the world champion motorcycle stunt jumper at 18 years of age, and have already earned him a fortune. He has performed feats that the 'experts' said were impossible because the risk of failure was too great. Quite undeterred, Eddie quietly prepared himself for the task and did it. Even when a film company required him to jump a 100ft-wide ravine without a crash helmet and with a dummy strapped on his back, Eddie weighed up the chances, then calmly and successfully took on this daunting task that no one else would even look at.

This, then, is the simple formula that can bring success with fun and happiness that has worked so well for thousands of other people. Follow their lead in reaching for your goal. You know what you want, you have the ability. Make your plan, then put it into action with single-minded determination and a refusal to be deterred or sidetracked by well-meaning people full of dire warning. All this other so-called 'advice' is the product of minds which envy your enterprise, minds which are not strong enough to impel their owners into similar action, and which accept mediocrity too easily.

Successful preparation

There are certain steps you must take to prepare yourself fully for going into business on your own, and these entail 'doing your homework'. Before you cast adrift from your present occupation, keep your lip buttoned. Some considerable time may elapse between making the momentous decision to strike out on your own, and the point where you take the fateful step of giving your notice to your employer. Telling your pals at work that you are thinking of starting on your own, or dropping hints to neighbours and friends, can stir up trouble and a groundswell of difficulties just at the time when you want to concentrate on your preparations. Your boss may learn of your intentions, and may either turn nasty, or badger you daily to change your mind if he doesn't want to lose your services. Friends and neighbours will continually pose questions 'What's it all about?', 'What are you going to do?', 'When are you going to start?', 'How are your plans progressing?'. And they will all be anxious to offer 'advice'. You can do without all these distractions, and the only advice you need is that supplied by the people you know can give you the answers you want. You will already have made certain that your immediate relations — parents, wife, etc. — are supporting you in the venture and that they will keep quiet on your behalf until your preparations are complete and your business is launched.

The next step to take is to write down in detail everything your plan comprises so as to ensure that you leave nothing out that may be vital to a successful launch. Anything that may be sloppy, or not properly and completely thought out at this stage, may jeopardise that success. It's not good enough to ressure yourself with the airy statement that you've got it all in your mind. It is the painstaking attention to detail, and putting it all on paper, that counts. Trying to keep it all in your mind only leads to confusion and omissions that can trip you up, so commit everything to paper, even though some things may appear to be too trifling to bother about. If they have appeared in your mind whilst you have been thinking about your plan it means they probably have some significance. Moreover, by committing your thoughts to paper, you are clearing your mind to give its full consideration to the next idea. Any successful businessman will tell you his aim is to have a clear desk, so he does his best to keep any clutter out of the way, otherwise he cannot concentrate on the important plans and decisions that should occupy his working time.

Start with analysing the talents that are going to be used in forwarding your plan. What are the positive aspects? How can these be used to benefit other prople, either by way of service, or offering them something that is better than they are already using? Are your reasons for wanting to start on your own strong enough? Have they a truly sound base? If the answers to these questions are positive, then you should not be short on confidence with which to implement your plans. The basic principles of business remain the same no matter what the business is. 'Doing business' is performing a service that has a commercial value whilst providing fun, happiness and profit for the businessman. Is your plan geared to these principles? Do you know what you are aiming at if you achieve success in the beginning? Let your goal be the highest summit that you can conceive, and nothing less.

The man who gets to the top quickest is the all-round man whose grasp of the whole gamut of business is good. Are you prepared therefore to study every aspect of your prospective business? You don't have to be a specialist in any other area than the particular one upon which your business is based. Specialists can be hired to take care of accounting, banking, auditing, etc., but you must understand the main principles of these areas. It is wise to join a trade association if such exists in your sphere, and take publications which deal mainly with your principal interests. Join the local Chamber of Commerce and attend meetings of businessmen where all aspects of business are discussed. Always bear in mind that knowledge is power. The more you learn, keep in touch with developments and be aware of business movements in this country and worldwide, the greater will be your ability to take advantage of opportunities for increasing your success and beating your competition. The present time is richer in opportunity than ever before. The most tempting plums are there to be gathered, so continually widen your horizons to bring all those fat plums within your reach.

If you follow these simple rules you can write your own ticket for whatever degree of success you want. The person who rises above the rest is familiar not only with every facet of his own business and the industry, but also with general economic trends and conditions. To coin a phrase, 'familiarity breeds content'. The rewards will more than justify the effort in acquiring the knowledge.

Taking the plunge

Having got to the point where you are completely satisfied that you have covered the whole of the groundwork, you are now ready to take the cold plunge into the unfamiliar waters of being your own boss. If your business is making something, then you will want suitable premises and sufficient capital to keep the business healthy for the time it takes to make and start selling your product at a profit. If you start in business as a middleman, i.e. buying from a manufacturer or wholesaler and reselling at a profit, you may need premises to hold stock and a sales area, whether it be a shop, or sales counter. You need capital to purchase the stock and furnish your premises, to keep you until such time as you are trading at a profit, and to enable you to purchase more stock as sales are made. You may be in profit at an earlier stage than the person who goes into manufacturing — as we say at the beginning of this chapter, it took David Brown 18 months before he had a product to sell — but your commitments for stock may be greater. If you set up in a business providing a service of any kind, your capital commitments may not be as great as the examples given above, but it may still be necessary to have premises of some kind to house your machines, or to provide space for a cafe, restaurant, petrol station, launderette, take-away, etc., and to keep your head above water for some months whilst your business becomes viable.

Each of the above categories is given individual attention later on, but the general principles remain the same; you will require capital and probably premises. If you have done your homework correctly and fully, you will know exactly what is required in both of these spheres. Do not burn your boats unless you have ensured that these vital assets are at your command. Nothing changes even if you are buying an existing business; in fact you may have to exercise greater care than commencing from scratch. This category is so fraught with pitfalls that I have devoted an entire chapter to it further on.

Provided you have a viable proposition that you can support in full detail, and can prove on paper at least that you are worth backing, finance can be raised from many sources. Let's start with the most obvious, the local bank. If you already have an account at the bank, you have easy access to the manager. He already knows your credentials, you have been a good client, although, perhaps, only a small one. Personal accounts at banks are usually small and kept open for the convenience of having a cheque book, bank card, etc. You may think your account is not going to help in getting a loan, but bank managers are very shrewd people and the movements in and out on your account tell him whether you are likely to be a good or bad risk. If you are a good risk, then he will undoubtedly be willing to lend you a few hundred pounds. If you have some security such as a mortgage, or wholly owned property, or a good insurance policy, he may lend you up to a couple of thousand pounds or more against your security. If your requirement is for a more ambitious scheme which may need £10,000 or more, your bank manager will refer you to a merchant bank, usually one that is partly, or wholly owned by the bank. You can approach a merchant banker on your own if you wish — you may have been recommended to one. What the merchant bank will insist upon before lending money to you is that your idea is fully viable in the first place and that there is potential for large-scale growth. They are not interested in a business that will just tick over and has little potential.

Development area boards are in a position to loan large sums, provide rent-free factories, and provide many more facilities at either no cost at all, or very cheaply. Again they must be completely satisfied that you have a viable proposition and that you can provide jobs on their trading estate. If you are starting a business in the country, particularly in craftwork, then COSIRA — may help you. This body — The Council for Small Industries in Rural Areas — was set up to stop the drift to the towns. They have a healthy, practical approach to the financing, marketing and publicising of small, rural firms' products. COSIRA arranges multi-firm exhibitions of wares and has a lively information service. Dennis Allen of Solar Designs, situated in the village of Deddington, Oxfordshire, says his success is solely due to the help that COSIRA gave him. In his own words: 'We were pounding pavements, selling our silver gate bracelets to individual jewellery shops until COSIRA (who also helped us find factory premises) advised us to concentrate on wholesalers and the big groups, and revise our price structure.' The information office of COSIRA is at Queens House, Fish Row, Salisbury, Wilts. The addresses and telephone numbers of their regional offices can be obtained from the *Yellow Pages*.

ICFC (The Industrial and Finance Corporation) has specialised since 1945 in providing loan and equity capital to private companies. Whilst this source of finance is very seldom available to people who are just starting up in business, it is very helpful to bear in mind once you have got established. Loans will normally be secured on assets and will be linked to a shareholding in the business.

Other sources available are loans from personal friends, or relatives, sales of your assets, such as a car, or house, but this last should be at the bottom of your list of possibilities for providing finance. Many people who are solidly convinced of their business destiny have done just that. Dr Michael Sinclair sold every asset he could including his house and car to get started in a hospital service business. He succeeded, but only after a period of intense struggle, working day and night to keep his infant business alive. Now he is group managing director of Allied Investments, a multi-million-pound public company which runs nursing homes and agencies in this country, whilst selling British medical skills and techniques all over the world.

Profit from the gap in the market

Dr Sinclair is a magnificent example of succeeding where so many others have gone before. He was acute enough to discern a gap in the market. The ability to do that, and to have a capacity for hard work with dedication and concentration on the main chance, are probably the two biggest assets a budding self-made millionaire can possess.

Tom Clark saw a gap in the market which he thought he could fill, and went about the job with enthusiasm, guts and nerve. At 35, he is the founder and chairman of Edenlite, a multi-million-pound business which specialises in garden buildings, including aluminium greenhouses. He says: 'When I started the company, *I was absolutely and totally determined I was going to succeed'.* His success is all the more astonishing when it is realised that he has had to overcome a severe physical disability. He contracted polio at the age of 14. This robbed him of the use of his legs. His determination has kept him out of a wheelchair, but he can only get around with the use of two sticks. After leaving school at 18, he got jobs in various firms as a trainee accountant, then went to Rio Tinto Zinc Corporation. He took an accountancy correspondence course in the evenings, but never qualified because he found the studying so tedious. Nonetheless, he succeeded in getting the job of personal assistant to the managing director. This he found interesting and a very useful experience. After a time, however, he became frustrated because various people submitted schemes which he considered excellent, but which were given scant consideration, and usually shelved.

One of the schemes put up by a consultant engineer was a proposal for an aluminium greenhouse. Like the rest, this was rejected by the board of management, but Tom Clark thought it had the makings of a good proposition. At that time domestic greenhouses were all wooden and the idea of an aluminium one was revolutionary. Tom saw there was a gap in the market waiting to be exploited. Commercial growers had already started using aluminium greenhouses and had proved their superiority over wood. What clinched the deal was that the price of aluminium was falling at that time, whilst the price of wood was rising.

He pursuaded two friends to put up £250 each, and with his own share of £250 he gave up his job at Rio Tinto and rented a disused maintenance bay behind a garage in Northwood Hills. The total space was only 1500 square feet. They built a portable office and lavatory inside the shell of the building. Shortly after starting, one of the partners got cold feet so Tom found the £250 needed to buy his share. To commence with, the other partner drilled holes in the aluminium and built the greenhouses, whilst Tom did all the selling of the finished product and bought the raw materials. As he says: 'We did it in that order. *I believe that in any kind of business, you've got to get your priorities right. Our priorities were to get the orders first, then order the materials, and to pay for them later at the end of the longest credit period the suppliers would allow.*' His first sales were all direct to consumers. Then, finding the greenhouses were accepted enthusiastically by the purchasers, he began to advertise in gardening magazines and the national press. He supplied each enquirer with a coloured, glossy brochure — in strong contrast with most of the black and white stodgy leaflets that passed for brochures at that time.

Turnover in the first year was £35,000; with starting-up expenses to come out of that, a small loss was made. A small profit was made in the second year with sales of £120,000. In 1970, three years after the start, the company moved to Witney in Oxfordshire and a rented factory of 8500 square feet. Tom Clark thought this was enough space to grow in for some years ahead, but within a year he was renting room in some of the town's derelict wool mills, and the staff had increased to 20 in the works plus a number of office staff. Tom's experience in accounting enabled him to break down the operation into its simplest components. This meant that the firm never burdened itself with expensive machinery. It bought the aluminium ready-cut and drilled; all that remained was to put the parts up in appropriate kits and despatch them to the customer. An arrangement was made for the glazing agents to despatch the glass separately direct to the customer.

In 1973 Tom bought out his remaining partner for £250,000, and moved into an 85,000 square foot factory in Swindon, built to his specification. In 1976 his turnover was considerably in excess of £5 million, and the firm had moved aggressively into export. The current export turnover is more than £1½ million and is growing fast. The firm can now be said to be worth several million pounds and is still wholly owned by Tom Clark. He says: 'When you start on your own account in your 20s, you don't think about making vast sums. *What you think about is the necessity of making a success of whatever you set out to do.*' He attributes his success to:

1   Having devised a product which filled a need and gave the best possible value for money.
2   Getting his priorities right.
3   Being totally convinced that what he was doing was right.

His final words were: 'The great thing about being in business for yourself is that it's exciting and great fun'.

Conserving your capital

Now you are at the point where you have got the finance you need, do not spend a penny more than is absolutely necessary on premises and plant. The examples I have quoted prove the point that money is to be used to generate profit, not to sink into prestige premises and expensive plant or machinery. If you must have premises, then choose the cheapest that is consistent with fulfilling your purpose. If a low-rated area will do, choose that in preference to a situation in a choice high-rated spot. If a property can be obtained very cheaply because it is in need of renovation, or stuck in the back of somebody's yard, then take it. Roll up your sleeves and put it into reasonable order. Buy second-hand timber to make shelves, partitions, or whatever is needed. Buy paint and any other necessary materials cheaply from a discount store. Discontinued colours, or ends of lines, can usually be bought at a fraction of retail price. It's at the start of your business that you want to grudge every penny you have to spend that will not generate profit. If it's not absolutely necessary, don't buy it, or use a very cheap substitute. Once the profits start rolling in is the time to plan for better premises — and then only if they help to generate more profit — and labour-saving machinery, or purpose-built racks for stock, or manufactured shopfittings, electronic accounting machines, etc.

Borrowed money, particularly, must be spent very carefully, because it is carrying a burden of interest on its back which must be paid to the source from whence it was borrowed. Fixed assets don't produce any profit. Only turnover will do that, so the more cash value you are turning over, the greater the profit. Forget the prestige and concentrate on the sales. If you can contract the manufacture of your new product to another firm, then do so. Haggle like the devil over the price, but if you've done your figurework right, you are assured of your profit without the necessity of buying machinery to make the thing yourself.

Don't buy transport either. In the first place, enquire from your supplier if he will deliver direct to your customer, if the article he is making for you is completely finished at his factory and packed ready for dispatch. If he has a country-wide delivery service for his own products, he may well agree to do this. There will be some charge, of course, but this will be cheaper than using your own transport. If this cannot be done because of the circumstances, i.e. you buy a semi-finished product from him and assemble and pack at your own premises, then employ a local transport contractor to deliver for you. The costs can be known beforehand and built into your total oncosts of manufacture plus overheads on which you base your selling price. Buying and running your own transport is very expensive indeed and should not be contemplated at the commencement of your business. You will have to use capital to buy vehicles, or enter into a hire agreement carrying a high rate of interest. You will have to employ drivers, pay for insurance, service and repairs. Breakdowns will cost the earth in lost time and a loss of service to your customer, affecting the precious goodwill you are striving to build up. Another bonus that accrues from using other people's transport is that you are covered against any damage that might occur in unloading and delivering to your customer. If your driver cannot work for any reason, you are in trouble, but the use of a contractor will obviate this. Later on when you are well established you may be in a position where it becomes a viable proposition to run your own transport, but don't let such a move enter into your calculations when you are planning to start on your own; it's too big a drain on your precious capital and too big a risk.

Where to get official help

There are a considerable number of official and private bodies whose main aim is to help the small businessman. Mr Bill Poeton, founder member of the Confederation of British Industry, has been the leading light in setting up the Union of Independent Companies. This is a pressure group of small businessmen with sections in parliamentary constituencies. The idea is to form delegations to attend the 'surgeries' that each member of parliament holds regularly in his constituency. The member is then lobbied to champion the small businessman at every opportunity in Parliament. To add emphasis, and to keep the pressure building up, every meeting is reported in the local press, hitting the member where it really hurts. This is of very great nuisance value and keeps the member on his toes. Since it started recently, the UIC has formed groups in 52 consituences and the movement is spreading rapidly. Independent businesses represent the largest proportion of labour in Britain — 39 per cent as against 37 per cent for public companies, 11 per cent for local and central government and 10 per cent for nationalised industries. That 39 per cent adds up to more than 9 million people. 'If we can get into every key constituency with discussions, then publicise these to the electorate, we are bound to become a very real voice for small independent business, in fact an alternative democracy', says Poeton. The CBI's London address is 21 Tothill Street, SW1. Mr Chris Meakin is in charge of the Small Business Section.

The Association of Small Businesses, World Trade Centre, London E1, has 1500 members nationwide, and councils in each economic region. It has an advisory committee which will sort out any difficulties with official avalanches of paper. The Institute of Directors, 116 Pall Mall, London SW1, may seem a rather august body, and somewhat above the man just starting on his own, but they too are very much alive to the problems of the small independent person, and they operate a library and advisory service. There are 52 Chambers of Commerce in the country and hundreds of Chambers of Trade, all of which disseminate information, offer advice and assistance in solving problems or finding sources of assistance and information. The Conservative Central Office at Smith Square, London SW1 have a Small Business Bureau and, still in Smith Square, the Labour Party will assist via Ministers Harold Lever and Bob Cryer who are sympathetic to the small businessman and are genuinely trying to do something to mitigate their troubles. The government-sponsored Small Firms Information Centres have a very good counselling service. The counsellors are not civil servants, but retired small businessmen who understand problems and can usually supply satisfactory answers. They are in Glasgow, Cardiff, Newcastle on Tyne, Manchester, Leeds, Nottingham, Liverpool, Luton, Birmingham, Bristol and Belfast. Their addresses and telephone numbers are in the *Yellow Pages*.

There is, therefore, no excuse for you to be short of knowhow before you plunge into the cold waters of independence.

All the essentials should now be complete, and fully understood, for you to start. You have the premises, if required, the cash and the ability. If you have a relative, or partner, who is going to share the work with you, don't think me unkind if I suggest that it would be very wise to be quite certain that they are as dedicated as you, willing to work as hard as you, will cheerfully undertake any task, however menial, to forward the business, and will make the same sacrifices as you, whilst acknowledging that you are the boss. Be sure that you have the largest share of the partnership, or limited company, no matter how much you trust your partner. The road to failed businesses is paved with people whose partners have let them down in all kinds of ways. Have the control of the venture firmly in your hands from the word go, so that if a partner defects, or lets you down in any way, the stability of the business is not affected. If your partner is a 'sleeping' partner, then be equally certain that the financial arrangement is drawn up in such a way that prevents a sudden withdrawal of financial support, or that such support is not so heavily weighted against you that you can be sunk if anything happens to your sleeping partner. A good solicitor should give you advice in this respect. Any uncertainties that exist at the start can affect your peace of mind and reduce your chances of success.

Operating on a small capital

There are ways of operating a profitable business without committing more than a small proportion of your precious capital. Philip Gower is a good example of a man who built up a £10 million company without much capital in only six years. His philosophy was to let other people finance his business and make his profits, without cost to himself. As a grammar school boy in Leeds, Philip was so uninterested in school subjects that he only got one 'O' level. He said: 'My teenage ambition was to make money'. When he left school, he got a job with a firm whose management structure was all wrong, so he learned the things *not* to do. At 24 he struck out for himself with a capital of just £1000. He knew he had found a gap in the market in which he was interested and set out to exploit it. He bought an old van and took tiny premises on the outskirts of Leeds.

His plan was simple, as all good plans are. He found a manufacturer of plumbing goods who would offer a preferential price for bulk buying of items in stock. Without actually buying these goods, Philip went out and found customers who wanted those items and who would be prepared to pay cash in 7 days for special discounts on bulk purchases. Because his overheads were very low indeed, and because he was only dealing in bulk supplies, he was able to work on a low gross profit of 10 per cent, and still finish up with a good cash profit for himself. He didn't need any more capital, because his customers paid on the dot to get the special discount terms, and he didn't need to have any stock, because he only sold what the manufacturer had on *his* shelf. In a very short time he was able to move on to bigger things. In 1970 he bought a kitchen furniture company from the liquidator for a song, and a big old mill at a giveaway price because no one else would touch it with a bargepole. Philip said: 'The potential was not just in the space, but in the road access. As the buildings are on a hillside, by splitting them horizontally, we have *three ground floors*. This was done by making entrances at each road level. *Simple, but no one else had thought of it!*'

At the age of 30, his group of companies were worth £10 million, of which he owned 99 per cent. He says: 'I have only been accepted by the local business community in the last two years. They could not believe we have grown at such a rate on such a tiny capital without chicanery. But we do not compare ourselves with others. Our philosophy is simplicity. Sophistication costs money, so we keep management and administrative costs to the minimum, and ours are very low indeed compared with others. This is where so many companies fail on profitability. They put prestige before profit. I think I would destroy my companies by following traditional business ways.'

Philip Gower is a perfect example of a man becoming a success because he had the belief in his own abilities and the dedication to put his ideas into practice, despite a poor education, no influence and only a tiny capital. He found a gap in the system and exploited it in such a way that it cost him little more than was necessary to supply the rock-bottom basic needs of starting a business. If Philip had gone about the job in the normally accepted way of doing business, he would have been finished in a month or two. The normal method used by plumbers merchants is to stock everything a plumber can possibly want, necessitating a large warehouse with all its overheads and labour, giving normal credit terms to customers and not bothering too much if they pay late, and finding and supplying every little component his customers demand. Gower saw the simple way through the gap left by conventional methods, and pursued it relentlessly, because he knew his methods would generate both goodwill and cash at the same time, so his inevitable success cost him nothing.

Profiting from the success of others

Can you learn a lesson from Gower's example, and do the same? Every manufacturer and wholesaler has goods that he is willing to sell at keen prices if he can dispose of them in bulk. He may even be happy to deliver for you under your label. Conversely there are always buyers who are looking for good deals where they can get a discount on bulk purchases that will give them an edge on their competitors. If they can get a tiny extra percentage discount, say 1¼ per cent, they will pay cash on invoice.

If, at the beginning, before you have established a credit rating with your supplier, you have to pay cash, you can squeeze a little extra percentage for yourself simply because you *are* paying cash. Later on the supplier will give you 21 days', or even 30 days' credit, and still allow you a settlement discount for paying within his terms. If he gives 2½ per cent for paying within 30 days, you will see that in 12 months this adds up to 30 per cent on your purchases for the year. Because you are operating at a small overhead rate, and are selling at a small percentage above your buying price, this discount can be the means of keeping you not only afloat, but supplying the capital you need for expansion. If your turnover is only around £5000 per month, then the 2½ per cent monthly discount you are getting on your purchases can amount to a sum around £1350 per annum.

Simple rules for success

If you have done your homework, you must be able to find suppliers and buyers who will cooperate with you and make your business successful. You have three simple criteria that *must* be maintained at all times:
1   The goods you offer must be right.

2   The price you ask must be right.
3   Delivery must be immediate, or meet your customers' requirements in this respect.

This last should be easy, because you are only offering goods that are available immediately from your supplier. *Never, never* be tempted to 'oblige' your customer by taking orders for goods that are not available from stock. He may use all his persuasion on you to try and get these lines, but if you fall for it, you will be sunk, for you may be certain that he cannot get them from his usual source of supply and is using you as a last resource. If you do take his order, you are on a loser to nothing, so use your charm to emphasise the super service you give him simply because you stick to your principle of only supplying lines that are in stock. He will appreciate the point.

It always pays to keep your eyes wide open for opportunities to make money without spending any of your capital. The formula is to find someone who wants to dispose of stock at a low price, and to find someone who is in the market for that commodity. Match a willing seller with a willing buyer and you have profit without cost to yourself.

Here is an example: a stationer in a Midlands town was expanding rapidly, opening up in several towns. Naturally, he had to stock these new outlets. A person in the trade who knew of this situation also learnt that a stationery and greeting card wholesaler he dealt with was wanting to dispose of around 100 gross of a discontinued line of greeting cards. A price of £200 for taking the lot in bulk was agreed. At that time they would have retailed for about 5p each. The normal trade discount would have been $33\frac{1}{3}$ per cent, with perhaps a further 10 per cent for quantity and settlement discount. The expanding retailer was phoned, congratulated on his progress and enterprise, and informed that if he would take this lot of good selling cards, he could have them at 50 per cent off retail price for cash on delivery. It was a deal he could not ignore, and he clinched it on the spot. The trader doing the deal then phoned the wholesaler with a definite order for the cards, and he agreed to deliver direct to retailer on his next van delivery into the Midlands. He was also persuaded to give an extra 5 per cent for payment in 7 days following receipt of his invoice. The cost of the bulk lot from the wholesaler was £200 less 5 per cent for 7 days' payment, and the retailer paid £360 gladly for goods which would sell at £720. The resulting profit to the trader was £160 without any cost to himself of any kind apart from a few telephone calls, plus a bonus £10 as an agreed settlement discount. Call the last item cheeky if you like, but it's this kind of wheeling and dealing which equates with success.

Make no mistake, this kind of dealing is going on all the time in every part of the country. Shrewd middlemen who have done their homework are making a great deal of money without risking their own. A word of warning here to those people who are attracted to a proposition offered to them to take an agency for goods of any sort. If the proposition entails spending money on stocking the goods at your home, or premises, don't take the agency. Many people have been wise after the event, having had their fingers badly burnt. Unloading stock for immediate payment on to an unwary prospective agent is an excellent way of getting rid of unsaleable goods, and many shady characters pursue this line of unsavoury business. On paper, and in advertisements and literature they turn out, the proposition appears to be foolproof and offers high profits to an 'agent' who is usually told that he needs no expertise in selling, or knowledge of the goods, because they sell themselves, or the public are falling over themselves to buy, or — and this is the biggest temptation of all — the supplier will send the agent loads of 'introductions' to people who have answered advertisements placed by the supplier nationwide.

One clause of the agency agreement will always be the mandatory purchasing of stock 'which you must have to satisfy the hordes of eager buyers whose names and addresses we shall supply'. Even if you adopt the attitude of asking to see people who are already happy and satisfied agents, so that you can satisfy yourself that the proposition is above board and can be worked successfully, you may fall into the trap of being referred to a phony 'agent' who has been planted for the very purpose of lulling your suspicions, and who will supply plenty of 'proof' of his success in his 'agency'. Don't be fooled. This was how the infamous 'Pyramid' fraud was perpetrated a few years ago and in many guises. Thousands of innocent people were relieved of their hard-earned money, and only a public outcry put a stop to the shady game. People are still falling for frauds of this nature where they are persuaded to part with their money in exchange for 'large profits for no effort'. If this were truly possible, do you suppose the promoters of the scheme would want to share it with outsiders? They work on the age-old principle that a 'fool is soon parted from his money'.

There is no substitute for the qualities I have told you are necessary for success. Nothing comes easily, so exercise your mind and talents to the full all the time, and follow your chosen path, refusing to be thrown off course by other people's advice, or get-rich-quick schemes that will tempt you from time to time.

One final exhortation before you start. Watch that you don't become a 'workaholic'. It is possible to become as addicted to work as it is to drink or drugs. The satisfaction you get from pursuing your successful path can be so exhilarating that you want it to go on for ever, morning, noon and night. You can think of nothing that can replace it, so you soon get to the stage where it is all bed and work, with no relaxation. There will be times when your plan entails working more than 10 hours a day to meet a deadline, but if you wish to live to a ripe old age and enjoy both your working life and your retirement, then relaxation must be given as important a part in your working budget as the work itself. Don't neglect your family, or the demands of your body and mind to rest and have a break. If your normal day can't be one of around 8 hours maximum, then it's time to get assistance. Your body and mind need regular freshening up, just as much as a car needs regular servicing, and you owe it to yourself and to those dependent upon you to keep bodily and mentally fit throughout your life.

Chapter 10

OVERCOMING STARTING-UP PROBLEMS

You now have the guidelines firmly established for starting your business. Once you are launched on the path of planned success, many snags and pitfalls can beset you. You may have chosen a very modest property in which to begin your business, but have you got the legal side tied up correctly? If you are leasing it from the owner, what sort of lease have you signed? Is it a fixed term of years, with rent reviews at 5- or 7-year intervals? Is a clause included in the agreement allowing you to break the lease amicably if you wish to leave the property and move elsewhere if you are expanding, at any time to suit your business needs? Being tied hand and foot to a fixed-term lease can cost a lot of money if you wish to move before a rent review becomes due and you don't want to be saddled with the present property you are occupying. You may have a demand for the rest of the term's rent and that could be a millstone around your neck.

With current legislation being so onerous, it is incumbent upon you to watch your step very carefully if the lease is 'fully repairing'. Before signing such a lease, make sure the building conforms with the Fire Precautions Act, and the Health and Safety at Work Act. Many an unwary businessman has been caught out by these Acts after taking a building on a fully repairing lease. This clause absolves the owner of the property of any liability to 'improve' the building in accordance with the requirements of the Act as interpreted by the local fire brigade and local authority officials. It is wise therefore to consult these two authorities with a view to getting either a clearance for the building, or to get the owner to incorporate into the building any improvement required by the authorities, before you sign a lease. The costs of having such work done can be horrendous and well beyond your means.

Insurance can be a subject of controversy. Some property owners will insure the building, with you responsible for insuring the contents, but some owners will insist on you paying them a sum which they say is for insuring the building. You, however, are not given the opportunity of negotiating a price for insurance yourself, so you have no idea as to whether the figure you pay is reasonable or not. Be quite certain therefore that you have got the best deal you possibly can, and that you have covered any eventualities that may arise and cost a lot of money during your tenancy. You may say, 'Oh, it's my solicitor's job to see that I am protected against these things, so I need not bother my head about them'. Famous last words which have been rued by many hundreds of bussinessmen. You must make very sure you have got satisfactory answers to all the questions I have mentioned above, and that no large costs can be made against you after you have moved in. Are all the supplies in good order? Electrical wiring, plumbing, heating, etc.?

Using professional advice

You must have an accountant appointed to audit your books. There is many a good accountant with a small personal practice who can devote time to you. He will advise you on the simple books you must keep to account for your day-to-day transactions and on your business and personal taxation. Being in a small way himself, his charges will be more modest than those of a large accountancy practice, and he will normally be available at all times to advise you on the problems that will constantly be cropping up. As your business grows, a good accountant can become a very good friend who can save you a great deal of money with his sage advice, particularly in respect of taxation.

Another person who can become a good friend and advisor is your bank manager. People tend to shy away from contact with a bank manager, as they do with tax inspectors, but keeping him fully informed of your plans and how you are progressing can be a very worthwhile exercise, for there are many ways in which he can — and will — help. He will, of course, be fully conversant with every type of financial facility available to businessmen, he can use the network of the nationwide banking scene to obtain information you may need of business and business people in any other area of the country. He can vet the credentials of new potential customers before you allow them credit, and can inform you of any general movement in your type of business that might possibly affect you for good or bad, and he can keep his sensitive finger on the pulse of your business to help you steer clear of pitfalls and help you to keep on the right track. All the information and knowledge you glean from him will increase your all-round knowledge of the business world in general and your own in particular, so cultivate his friendship and pay heed to his advice.

Controlling credit and bad debts

As pointed out in Chapter 9, there are ways of doing business without using your own money. If you can utilise any of these methods, or successful variations of them, do so. Giving credit, however, is a subject that must be handled very carefully indeed, particularly at the start of a business when every customer is a new one. Bad debts are the bane of most businesses, just as much as pilfering and shoplifting is the bane of the stores which sell for cash. Most stores build a percentage for theft into their annual budgets, but if you are to be competitive, the prices you will have to charge may not allow for the contingency of bad debts. Many small firms have gone to the wall a year or two after starting because they have been far too trusting. All businesses are out to get the longest credit they can, so if you can fix your period of credit at less than the period your suppliers allow, do so ruthlessly. If you can build up a circle of clients who are very happy to pay in, say, seven days, for a discount, you will be safe financially, provided the discount is allowed for in your profit margin. You may be able to double your business quickly by giving long credit, say 30 or 60 days, but this may deprive you of working capital. Moreover, it only needs the grapevine to start working in your trading area for your clients and potential clients to realise that you are an easy touch for credit. Giving long credit, even with no discount, will produce a difficult, financial embarrassment in the short run, but keeping a very tight reign on your customers, whilst allowing them a settlement discount, will conserve and increase your capital, allowing you to plough money back into expanding the business.

It is a paradox that the longer credit you give, the worse your bad debt situation is. Turn your face firmly against giving long credit in order to get large orders. In asking for such long credit, your potential client is testing the waters. Such orders are very tempting bait, but his ploy must be resisted at all times for the end result must be disaster. Emphasise the advantages you are offering if you make the sale, but make it clear that you could not offer such an attractive package if the deal included long credit. Chasing bad debts is a nerve-wracking job and not only wastes money, but valuable time. The resulting mental strain can affect your ability to keep yourself on top of form for running the business. If you hive the debts off to a debt-collecting agency, the costs are quite high, and can prove quite a drain on your resources. Moreover, even the most efficient of these agencies cannot collect 100 per cent of your outstanding debts. You run such risks as lie in the time factor involved. You allow one or two weeks to pass over the credit limit before you start chasing the debt, or pass it to the agency, so two months or longer may elapse after the date of invoice before some action is commenced. By this time your chances of collecting the debt have decreased significantly. Your client may be in bad shape financially, or even bankrupt, and you may lose your money completely, whereas if you had taken action before you might have recovered the amount of the debt. Contact your client immediately he goes over the credit limit by just one day. Call on him if possible, so that you can collect a cheque personally, or telephone him to ensure that a cheque is in the post to you. When you make these requests for payment be polite but very firm that your bill must be settled immediately. If payment is not forthcoming straight away, then it will be necessary to write to your client stating that the debt payment is overdue and that strong action will be taken if the account is not settled in three days.

The best action to take at this point — and the cheapest in the long run — would be to wait 24 hours after sending your letter to ensure that the client has received it, then to call on him personally. If, at this point, he uses some excuse to put off paying you, you may be quite certain he is not worth retaining as a customer for future business, and you must employ the strongest tactics you can to force his hand into signing a cheque. Inform him, if the debt is below £100, that you will get a court order against him with costs, *or* that you will get your solicitor to recover the debt with costs. There are a series of simple actions that can be taken through your local County Court, and the officials there will be very helpful in explaining the various simple procedures, right up to sending in the bailiff. The fees are not high, and nothing like the cost of employing a solicitor.

There are, unfortunately, a significant number of very large firms who deliberately delay payment to suppliers. They use their big power to cow the small supplier with an implied threat that they will lose business if they insist on payment to terms. Unless you can load your invoices to take care of this ramp, you would be better off without such clients as they can tie up too much of your valuable capital. It is a fact that many small businesses have become bankrupt because they have been unable to obtain payment of their accounts to a large client. It is tempting to supply such people, but the consequences may be horrific. Ask other firms in your line what their experience is with that firm before you start doing business with them. If such information is not available, get an assurance from the purchase accounts department of the potential large client that they do, as a matter of principle, pay to terms. Be quite frank with them when you make such an enquiry, and tell them that you are not in a position to give longer credit than you state on your invoices and statements. As there is no question of them not having the finance to pay to terms, it might be to your advantage to offer them a small discount for earlier settlement. If your normal term of credit is 30 days, they will be keen to take 1½ per cent discount for payment in 10 days. They appreciate fully that 1½ per cent per month equals 18 per cent per annum, and they are not going to turn that down if it is offered to them. Whatever you do *never deviate from your fixed credit terms* and be suspicious immediately if you are asked for an extension of payment. It's your money these people are using, and it's better being used in your business than in theirs. Even if people pay regularly, but always late, then either reduce the amount of business you are doing with them, or cease trading with them altogether.

Keeping good business relations

Conversely, do not pay your own suppliers a day before necessary, but always adhere to their terms of credit. It is far better for business relations for you to be regarded as a good credit risk rather than one who is on the borderline because you occasionally pay a little late. In this context, I must emphasise once again that as a good credit risk, you are more likely to obtain extra discounts, or settlement discounts, and you will be first in line for those special offers that suppliers give from time to time. Being on good terms with your suppliers can be worth its weight in gold to you, whilst delaying payment of their accounts can lose you far more than you may realise. As your business grows, there may come an opportunity to request an exclusive agency for certain goods. In other words, you are granted the valuable opportunity of being the only distributor in your particular territory, with no competition from outside. It is only a cast-iron business integrity that will get these extremely valuable concessions, and a vital part of this integrity is the recognition that you always pay to the suppliers' terms.

One of the things not to do which will be pointed out by your friendly bank manager, and possibly your accountant, is to overtrade. It may seem silly not to take all the orders you can possibly get for the largest possible amounts, but you can do too much business and go bust, in the same way as doing too little business. You must always operate within your financial limitations, and your accountant can lay down guidelines for you in this respect. Doing too much business — i.e. overtrading — can stretch your finances to breaking point before you realise what is happening. Too much money is tied up in stock and credit to clients, with the result that you cannot pay your own suppliers in their credit time limit, and your bank manager will not be inclined to lend you money when you are in this situation. Nor will any other source of finance. If you already have an overdraft facility at the bank and cannot offer security for an extension above it, you are either sunk, or you have to take drastic steps that can lose you both money and business integrity. Those steps must be:

1   A quick sale, for cash, of some stock; and
2   A request to your clients for payment of your invoices before the credit time you allow.

The first will lose money for you, because you will have to sell at or below cost to get that quick cash sale. The second will throw doubts upon your business standing, as your clients will quickly come to the conclusion that you are in deep financial trouble. This will cause doubts in their minds regarding continuing to trade with you, because you may be in no position to supply their orders.

If you are driven in desperation to request an extension of credit from your suppliers, then you are in the process of building your own business coffin. Some suppliers will certainly stop delivering to you, and the news that you are in financial trouble will travel round the trade like wildfire. Suddenly you will find all kinds of excuses will be made from all quarters for not filling your orders. Overnight you will be regarded as a bad business risk, and your integrity will have disappeared like snow in summer. A carefully drawn budget will include the maximum amount of turnover you must achieve in the year ahead, and it would be suicidal to exceed this amount of business. Monitor your turnover month by month so that your financial resources are always in a healthy position. The only allowable exception to this rule is when you sell for cash, or on a payment basis not longer than 10 days, or half the credit limit allowed by your own supplier.

Government regulations

Another starting-up problem may be posed by the sheer weight of government Acts and Regulations. Two have already been mentioned, the Fire Precautions Regulations and the Health and Safety at Work Act. Others which may affect you and your business are the Contracts of Employment Act, The Equal Pay Act, The Race Relations Act, The Sex Discrimination Act, The Redundancy Payments Act, The Trades Union and Labour Relations Act and The Employment Protection Act. Copies of these Acts can be obtained from many sources such as solicitors, some libraries, government stationery offices, etc. There is no room in this book to elaborate on the impact of the various Acts on business generally, for that would need a book of its own, but it is very wise to keep yourself informed of the provisions of the Acts and how they affect your particular business. In law, ignorance is no excuse. As these Acts touch upon everything you do in business, and it is so easy to fall foul of their provisions, it should be required reading for you to either find out for yourself, or get advice, how they can affect you, and what precautions you can take to avoid infringing these Acts. As mentioned in an earlier chapter, the Tribunals set up to implement the provisions of the Employment Protection Act have the power to fine an offending employer up to £11,500 for any one offence. Even if a case is settled out of court, the costs can be crippling to a small businessman.

When you start up, or very shortly afterwards, you will have to make up your mind whether to register for VAT or not. If your business totals £10,000 per annum or over, it is mandatory to register. You may begin in a very small way, and your build-up to that figure may be slow. What do you do in the meantime? Being registered for VAT has certain advantages, inasmuch as you can claim VAT back on all your purchases which have a VAT content. This includes things like petrol and oil, cars, vans, petty cash items, and anything you use in your business such as stationery, business machines, fixtures and fittings, etc.

You will see, therefore, that as you purchase so many items at the start of a business which have an element of VAT, it is possible to lose quite a large sum if you are not registered from the day you start up. Customs and Excise are very helpful in the advice they can offer if requested. You are furnished with the various VAT books showing which items are subject to VAT and at what rates, and what kind of category you can register in according to the type of business you operate. The returns which are rendered quarterly are very simple.

The VAT content of your purchases and sales — inputs and outputs as the form calls them — are entered on the form, and the difference between them is the amount you either pay to Customs and Excise, or qualify for a credit payment from them. This last is always made direct to your bank, never in the form of a cheque to you. It is, therefore, at the start of a business that a credit against your purchases for the VAT content can be an important saving. Apart from VAT on fixtures and fittings, vehicles, etc., it may be necessary to build up a stock before you can start selling. The VAT credit after your first quarter's trading can amount to several hundred pounds and can tide you over a period when you are earning little or nothing. As you see, if you don't register for VAT, there is no way you can get this back on your purchases. Later on, when your business is established, you may decide that it is no longer worth being registered, but that is a business decision only you can make. You will have to have either a separate VAT account book, or devote a section of an account book to that purpose, i.e. to register the inputs and outputs, and to file the appropriate invoice copies of your VATable sales and purchases, for these must be available at all times for examination by the Customs and Excise officers.

Your Customs and Excise officer can be a very good friend, but he won't be best pleased if he calls upon you and finds he has to go through all your books to separate the inputs and outputs from all your other transactions, so do keep separate accounts for VAT purposes.

Finding customers

How do you find customers? If you are opening a shop, you will have planned well beforehand how you are going to attract custom into the shop. A good layout, stock displayed to catch the eye, price labels displayed, special items highlighted, a bright attractive window display and a cheerful, helpful attitude from your shop assistant, or from yourself if it's a one-man show. Advertising in the local paper, leaflets distributed to houses in the vicinity of the shop, or to local businesses if you are selling to this category of customer, special opening offers, and/or discounts. All these will bring customers in.

You can get professional assistance *without cost* for window displays, by making a request to your suppliers, for a good window display featuring their goods is valuable advertising for them. It is even possible to get financial assistance from suppliers on advertising costs. In many cases they will handle the advertising completely and take space in the paper, charging you a proportion of such costs. Many shrewd businessmen have taken full pages in the paper, then offered space to their suppliers at a shared cost. Full pages attract the best amount of business and suppliers are usually eager to take space in such a campaign. The advertising editor of the paper will usually agree to write an editorial on your business to accompany your full-page advertising; this is excellent free advertising for you. This kind of advertising can be repeated from time to time as circumstances dictate and favourable opportunities occur. Advertising should be continuous if the biggest total impact is to be made, but it need not take more than two per cent of your budget once you are established.

If you open a factory or warehouse, or start a service business, you can only make sales by appealing direct to the business user of your goods or services. You do not have a shop in which to display your wares, so you have to beard your potential customer in his own den. Unless the proposition is very attractive, it is extremely difficult to persuade businessmen to leave their offices or premises to spend valuable time in looking at your factory or warehouse. When you get established, and the goods you are selling lend themselves to it, you may open a trade counter on your premises where the client can pick up his requirements.

Starting out, however, usually means legwork. You can soften the difficulties and open doors by judicious advertising before opening, in a similar fashion to the shopkeeper. Letters, leaflets, brochures can be sent to potential customers. If you can find the name of a person in these businesses to whom the literature can be addressed, then do so. It will receive more attention than if it were just addressed to the firm. In the latter case much of your efforts may be wasted, because your costly material might never reach the person you really want to contact. Instead, it finishes up in the wastepaper basket. Back up your literature with telephone calls to fix appointments with the man who can buy your goods or services. The telephone operator will usually give you his name if you don't already know it. Simultaneously with this, advertise in the appropriate paper, again taking a full page if possible with help from your suppliers, followed up by continuous advertising at a figure not greater than two per cent of your budget. Trade fairs and exhibitions can be valuable means of showing and selling your attractive wares or services.

How do you make a successful sale when you are face to face with your prospective buyer? Let us say straight away that there is an art that can easily be cultivated in selling successfully. Many people equate the successful salesman with the aggressive salesman, the man who forces his personality on his prospect with his dynamic approach and who obliges his client to give him the order in preference to a competitor. Such a man may burn brightly for a short time and his order book may be full, but he must fail sooner rather than later because he has not studied the psychology of good salesmanship. A buyer does not look upon such a person as being a superman at all. To him a salesman is someone who uses all kind of wily tricks to put one over on him, and so his defences are permanently up.

The more aggressive a salesman is, the more defensive the buyer becomes. The aggressive salesman may enjoy engaging in a battle of wits with his prospect. On his first call he may even get a good order, but it may well be his last because the buyer will resent the methods he has used. The primary object of the buyer is to buy benefits for his company, not just simply goods, so the salesman must use all his knowledge and training to persuade the buyer that he will benefit by buying the goods. If you always bear this in mind when you are face to face with a buyer, and you can genuinely show that you can offer something that will benefit him, you are on the road to success without the necessity of being aggressive or pushing in any way. Thus your clients become your friends and you will have established a bond that is lined with gold, for you will get preference when they are placing orders. If you just let people know what you have to offer with a view to finding out if the goods or services are genuinely needed by, and can benefit the prospect, you are surmounting the barrier between you and the result will be satisfactory to both sides, with the buyer looking forward to your next visit.

When meeting a prospective buyer for the first time, tell him you would like to be of service to him if he is in need of what you have to offer, and ask if you could talk to him about it — a very simple, direct approach which will get results, because it is refreshingly different from the usual tactics used by most salesmen which puts the buyer on the defensive. Selling should not be a contest between the two sides. Your training, knowledge of your goods, and competence is available along with the goods themselves to help and benefit the buyer and his firm. Give him your undivided attention, listen carefully to what he has to say, ask his opinion, show that you genuinely value his knowledge of the subject. Many buyers are regarded as very hard men who put the fear of God into salesmen, but the hardest of them likes being with people who will listen to them with interest, and who are friendly and concerned with their needs and their problems. The battle of wits is converted into an agreeable exchange of views and ideas. You can congratulate yourself when a buyer says it is a pleasure meeting you and doing business with you. Keep your selling philosophy on these lines and that valuable business is yours for keeps without fear of competition pushing you out.

Successful purchasing

The same tactics apply when you are buying from a salesman for your own business, but in reverse. You will be able to judge the value of a salesman's efforts to get your business, without prejudice, and make a cool assessment of the value and benefit you might get from the lines he is offering. Give him your attention and listen carefully to what he has to say. You can learn something new every day that can be of benefit to you. Far too many buyers refuse to see salesmen and so they miss many opportunities of hearing about new lines, new developments, new, young, lively firms with good offers. They deny themselves the privilege of enlarging their knowledge, and they do their own firms a grave disservice. It is unfortunate that a category of buyers exists that always gives orders to the same salesman, and will not even see a salesman from a competitive firm. How can they judge if they are right in continuing to buy from the same firm if they have no comparisons to call in judgement? How can they justify continuing to hold down their job when they are both incompetent and lazy? They will never benefit their firm with new improved goods, or get a better deal, and management would be better off without them.

If you have absorbed these lessons you should have fewer problems than average when starting in business, and you should have all the necessary ammunition to achieve success.

Chapter 11

BUYING A BUSINESS

Buying a business that has been run by someone else must be a gamble. Are you willing to weigh up all the chances of that gamble being a winning one? There are a great many questions to ask before you sign the contract for purchase, and the answers to those question must be in the affirmative. Many people have bought businesses on the spur of the moment for many reasons other than cold logic. A shop may be situated in an area which attracts, or it may be a pretty place, or the owner may be a charmer. Others have thought they have covered everything that might go wrong and then discovered that somewhere along the line one or more major setbacks occur that were not taken into consideration before purchase.

The person most likely to succeed is the one who knows

the business or trade better than the seller, who knows all the angles to running that type of business, and has confidence in himself to create his own success. If you have to start to learn from scratch, with just a few tips from the previous owner, or working for a week or two under his supervision, you are in for a big unpleasant surprise when you are left on your own. Most of the problems you encounter will need experience of the trade to overcome them. Without that experience you have little chance of weighing up the situation and arriving at the correct answer. It is possible to make glaring mistakes when you *are* experienced, so what chance has the novice at the game? Hundreds of retired servicemen, repatriated colonials, people with some savings who are fed up with their job have 'fancied a little business of my own', and have sunk all their savings into purchasing a shop.

The favourites are usually a village shop, with newspapers and sweets, craft shop, small boutique, antique shop, country cafe or small hotel, etc. They may have been very successful at their previous calling, but that does not provide them with the experience or knowledge of the innumerable snags encountered in running a business. The cost of innocence can be frightening and often ends in the bankruptcy court with the stunned bankrupt repeating over and over to himself 'What went wrong?'. There are still safe investments that can offer a return of over 10 per cent. These people would have been far wiser to have made such an investment, leaving their capital in safe hands and receiving a reasonable living, than to have plunged blindly, with all their hard-earned capital and rose-coloured spectacles, into a business.

The principal purpose of this chapter is to provide the safeguards that can help you avoid the main pitfalls laying in waiting.

Safeguards against failure

Start with 'checklists of' questions that must be answered clearly, coldly, and to your own unbiased satisfaction:

Personal	Yes	Don't Know	No
Do I realise that running a business means very hard work?			
Can I get along happily with people?			
Can I resolve unpleasant situations when they occur?			
Am I willing to work for a pittance until I am sure of success?			
Have I the ability to plan ahead and budget?			
Have I the right basic knowledge of the business?			
Am I afraid of taking risks?			
Am I able to sell to people?			
Can I understand simple accounts?			
Am I really going to be happy in my own business?			
Is my wife, or partner, going to enjoy working in this type of business?			
Have I the basic capital to start and to keep going?			

If your answers are in the affirmative, and you have not kidded yourself over any aspect, then you should be ready to actively seek the kind of business you want. Which leads to the next list:

Before the business is bought	Yes	Don't Know	No
Have I looked into the proposition from *every angle?*			
Have I asked the opinion of people who have had dealings with the business, and with customers?			

	Yes	Don't Know	No
Have I spent enough time with the owner of the business to be sure of his *bona fides?*			
Have I investigated his financial position?			
Have I asked why he is selling the business, *and got the right answers?*			
Am I satisfied that the business is showing a good profit *that is genuine?*			
Is the level of profit as good as or better than similar businesses?			
If there are employees, are they the right type and, if so, will they stay on?			
Do I know all the problems that beset this type of business?			
If there are problems, will I know how to solve them?			
Is the current business and financial climate suitable for the continued success of the business?			
Has the business and position a good future potential for growth?			
Does this type of business suit my personal qualities?			
Are my solicitor and accountant totally satisfied with the purchase contract?			
Will I have sufficient capital left to run the business successfully after paying for the purchase?			
Can I cut the overheads and increase the profit?			

	Yes	Don't Know	No
Will this business give me the success I am looking for?			
Am I absolutely certain the vendor is not selling a dud business by concealing unsavoury facts about it?			

Financial considerations

	Yes	Don't Know	No
Can I get the additonal capital I need?			
Will my bank manager offer finance?			
Can I give him acceptable security for the loan?			
Can I afford the interest on the loan?			
Can I find another source that will cost less?			
Will the business earn enough profit to pay the loan back in time and leave sufficient for interest, as well as give me a living?			
Would the owner be willing to take his purchase price in instalments, or leave part of the price in the business where it would cost me less than bank interest?			
Is there some stock in the business that could be sold to produce cash, without harming the future of the business?			
Could I pay off the loan if the business failed?			

Once you have purchased the business, you are faced with another set of vital questions:

Management considerations	Yes	Don't Know	No
Have I a warm and friendly personality that will be attractive to customers?			
Is the place in good order, neat and tidy?			
Is all the equipment and fixtures and fittings in good shape?			
Is the exterior attractive to the public? Are the outside signs and lighting OK?			
Will customers be comfortable in the place?			
Is the business stationery impressive?			
Are the staff trained to be courteous and efficient?			
Is the display of goods attractive?			
Do I know when to allow and when to refuse credit?			
Are prices right to give the profit margin I want?			
Are the prices competitive with similar businesses?			
Are the goods clearly marked with the price?			
Do I know all there is to know about the business, and am I always willing to learn more?			
Do I take all the relevant trade magazines so that I can keep up-to-date with prices and trends?			
Is my advertising good, adequate, and in the right media in the best position?			
Am I prepared to analyse my advertising to see which pays best?			

	Yes	Don't Know	No
Do I distribute leaflets and other literature to my customers, and use mail order?			
Am I planning for growth, in both the long and short term?			
Am I constantly looking for better ways of buying, and getting better discounts?			
Am I training someone on my staff to run the place efficiently if I am ill or on holiday?			

Three long lists that can spell the difference between success and failure, so regard them as absolutely essential. Take a great deal of time and care in answering each and every one of the questions. The right answers can be worth their weight in gold. Don't try and kid yourself that you already know it all, so there's no need for bothering about matters such as those raised in the questionnaires. Don't think, either, that you can afford to spend time on leisure pursuits during working hours in the fond hope that your staff or assistant can run the business perfectly well in your absence, and without your personal supervision.

Safeguarding the cash

Another essential 'must' is the daily monitoring of the finance of the business, and a simple but accurate weekly balance sheet. If you were wise you would have made a budget at the beginning of the year, or before you opened the business, aimed at producing a satisfactory profit at the end of the year. It's no use at all having a vague idea from time to time that things are progressing well, and then waiting for your accountant to produce the annual balance sheet showing what profit, if any, you have made during the past year. You may have been working your fingers to the bone during that time, but hundreds of hard-working small businessmen have gone under because they did not take the elementary precaution of using an hour or two of their evenings once a week to keep tabs on their financial position. If you don't know, or have only a vague idea, how you are progressing, how can you be ready to face up to the unknown, or unexpected big problem that suddenly confronts you? How can you reasonably accept or refuse the tempting offer that is made, if you don't really know whether or not you can afford the outlay at the particular time?

Buying the right shop

There are a few more important points you should learn when looking for a suitable shop to buy. Hundreds are always available, and are usually advertised in the local and national newspapers and in specialised journals catering for the particular trade required. Most house and property agents have a few businesses for sale on their books, and in the larger centres there are specialist business transfer agents.

The technique to adopt when you meet an agent is to be cool, give the impression you know exactly what you are talking about (having done your homework thoroughly before you start looking, I hope), and know just what you want — size, type, location, profit, etc. Never let yourself appear to be anxious and eager to do a deal, but on the other hand don't give the agent the impression that you are only there to waste his time, and that you really have no idea what you want. If he thinks you are a genuine potential buyer, he will be very happy to answer all your questions and to show you the shops in which you display interest. Eventually — and this may be after seeing a number of agents in different locations — you will see a shop that attracts you more than others.

Because you want plenty of customers, is the shop in a densely populated area, or a rich area? A shop in an isolated village of a few hundred souls may be picturesque, but it is unlikely to make you a good living. There may be a lot of people about, but observation should tell you whether or not they are calling at the shop, or just using the street as a route to the supermarket or the town centre. It is vital that you spend one or two days, preferably a normally busy day, and an average day, to count the number of people patronising the shop. There's no need to make yourself conspicuous whilst performing this task. Don't be afraid of competition from similar shops to your choice, because superior management will always win the battle of competition. If you are in what is known as a prime area, the shop should be very busy. Being next door to a supermarket, Woolworths, Marks and Spencers, Boots, etc., puts you right in the heart of the buying section. If it is a newsagents and sweet shop, the above still applies, as does a location next to a busy bus or railway station. This wealthy location will undoubtedly mean that the price of the business may be much higher than any other, and the rates — and rents if you are renting the premises — will be high because of the prime position. You will have to do your sums in this case. You can be absolutely certain of having a busy shop and a higher turnover than in any other location, but will the turnover generate the necessary profit?

It is a melancholy fact that many a good, profitable one-man business in a prime location has had to be disposed of because the escalating rates and rents have made the operation unprofitable, simply because the shop cannot operate on the same scale of turnover per square foot as the multiple. You can take it for granted that the rates will increase each year by around 10 per cent; in a prime area this can mean a large sum. Can you increase your *net* profit by about £2 or more per week just to take care of the increase in rates? If the shop in which you are interested is on lease, then make sure the lease has more than 12 years to run. If the lease is short and falls in when you are the tenant, the required increase per annum of a new lease may well put you out of business just when you are getting established. Besides, a long lease has a value when you are selling. You may want to move on in a comparatively short time, and that lengthy lease can be worth a few thousand pounds when you sell.

If the shop you are buying keeps open during conventional hours, i.e. 9 a.m. to 5.30 p.m., a great deal of extra profit could probably be extracted from the business if you extended the opening hours, say from 8.30 a.m. to catch the early morning shopper or passer by on the way to work, to 8 p.m. Many households have both adults at work during the day, and will patronise a convenient shop which stays open in the evening. The same applies at week-ends when the big shops are closed. Thousands of small shops stay profitable because they cater for this class of trade. If you are not prepared to work these long hours, perhaps you should follow Sir Harold Wilson's injunction to a Minister: 'If the heat in the kitchen is too much for you, then get out of the kitchen'. Lasting success *always means hard work.* There's just no way around it. Slogging away at a job, whether it's for yourself or for an employer, is the only way to earn for yourself a later easy life with no worries.

If you buy the business you are interested in, does it have room for expansion? Is any part of the premises other than the shop itself available for enlarging the shop area? Is there a room which has been used as a kind of rest-cum-teabreak room? Perhaps there is a room, or space at the rear, which has been used for housing stock? It will always pay you to look ahead in this fashion because you would hardly be buying the business if you didn't want to expand.

Spotting the potential profit

Many people have made fortunes in a comparatively short time by buying a shop or business, using their expertise and management talents to improve the turnover and profitability quite dramatically, then selling at a figure twice or three times what they paid, yielding the capital required to repeat the performance. The trick is to spot the situation with potential, where poor management has resulted in a run-down business, or where the owner has got financial troubles which entail a quick disposal of the business at a knock-down price. With all the other signs right, the change in favour of the new owner can be dramatic. Get the formula right and you must win. If the situation is good, the potential trade OK, the overheads low in comparison with the potential, the premises capable of being made far more attractive at a budgeted cost, with the only wrong thing being the owner or manager, then you are on a winner to nothing. The formula is simple, so by keeping within your proven guidelines, the business can be bought at your figure, action can be swift, and the turnround to a successful, profitable business dramatically achieved. It has been known for a person to turn an original capital of less than £1000 into £100,000 and more in a space of five years by shrewdly using this formula to buy shops, build them into profitable enterprises quickly, then sell, and repeat the process on an increasing scale as his capital grows.

A footballer playing for a club in the North-West was badly injured on the football field and had to retire from the sport in his 20s. He used his compensation money in following the above formula, concentrating on small discount stores. He quickly built up a successful chain, and has now sold out to a large supermarket firm for a sum in excess of £1 million. There is no secret, or luck, about his success. A combination of hard work, plus the formula, must result in the achievement of the result you planned for.

Avoiding loss or theft

One warning and one caution: If you are going into the above type of business enterprise, don't buy businesses with a home attached. For one thing your wife and family will resent constant moves; for another a house doesn't generate profit. So only concern yourself with a shop or business with premises, the total area of which is, or can be, used to generate profit.

The caution concerns managers and staff. If left totally in charge, without supervision, it is very tempting to staff to slip cash into their pocket instead of the till, and to be somewhat free in their interpretation of what perks comprise, particularly where shelf stock is concerned. A bad habit of taking the odd packet, or item, for their own purpose can soon escalate into outright theft. Supervision and constant random checks are essential if you are to avoid considerable losses. Professional crooks move about the country representing themselves as qualified managers. They are armed with all the essential papers, such as good references; their impeccable manners and knowledge of the trade, their charm and air of respectability, all ensure that they have no trouble in getting appointed, and the owner is quickly lulled into complete acceptance of their 'integrity'. The result is that, once they are left to run the place without supervision, they take the first opportunity of disappearing with all they can carry away, both cash and stock. The moral of this story is never to accept total strangers at their word, but to employ people who are already known to you. If you do suffer a loss of this nature, the chance of getting anything back is practically nil. Whilst, on investigation, you find they are already known to the police, it will cost you far too much to pursue the matter of prosecuting them and attempting to get your money back. You can only write it off to experience.

Chapter 12

MORE AIDS TO SUCCESS

First, two more case histories which have real lessons for those who are ambitious for themselves, and hope for those in despair of ever rising from the depths.

The mass tea markets of this country are supplied by about four principal tea blenders, Brooke Bond, Typhoo, Lyons and the Co-op. Between them they were able to establish prices which gave them a good profit and secured the market against anyone else trying to muscle in. Not quite, but almost a monopoly. John Loveridge, a Norwich man with family connections in the grocery trade, spotted the gap in the market waiting to be exploited by someone with the knowledge of the trade. A firm of small tea blenders in Norwich was on the rocks, and John snapped them up at a knock-down price. He then proceeded to buy his tea in the same bulk tea markets as the big boys, and in competition with them. Because of his low overheads combined with his expertise, he was able to blend a fine tea which could undercut the elephants of the trade by around 10p a quarter. His pack was attractive, and he gave it the trade mark of Mecca Tea. He was able to offer the retailer a good margin of profit and, as the quality of his tea was equal to the competitive nationally known brands, he was soon selling all he could process. So successful was his enterprise that he was able to take much larger premises and install new machinery a few months after he had commenced.

Then the large supermarket chains such as Sainsburys began to sit up and take notice of the success of Mecca tea, with the result that John Loveridge is now looking forward to a turnover of £5 million per annum, with the sky as the limit. Although the Price Commission took a close look at the prices charged by the big blenders and insisted that their retail price be brought down from around 27p per quarter to about 22p, and was met with stubborn opposition, John was still sitting pretty with his Mecca tea selling for about 17p a quarter. The principal tea blenders did their best to convince the Price Commission that they just could not afford to cut their price, but were still told to get on and do it, unless they were willing to pay stiff penalties. Undoubtedly, with their tremendous overheads, and cost of selling and advertising, they would find it difficult to cut their prices. John just goes blithely on, without the burden of big overheads, and will continue to grow and prosper. This case history illustrates once again that opportunities to find gaps in the market are there all the time, and they provide a golden path to fortune.

Desmond Douglas, a 22-year-old Jamaican, was brought up in dire poverty in Birmingham. With his parents, two sisters and a brother, he lived in a derelict house in the city, and gnawing hunger was always their companion. Desmond grew up to be a rootless teenager roaming aimlessly around the city. He had ambitions to be a bricklayer, but as he was left-handed, this came to nothing. He began to spend time in a YMCA hall which had table tennis tables, and where he had to beg for games. What practice he did get enabled him to develop a loose-wristed, flowing game with his left hand; he steadily improved until it was difficult to find anyone who could really test him. The club entered him for competitions at which he was invariably successful. Steadily he rose to being chosen to play in national competitions and his game improved all the time. With his continuing success in competitions came the inevitable invitation to play for the English team. Beating world-rated Hungarians, and in brilliant form in the European Championships, has brought him a contract to play for the big German club, Borussia Dusseldorf which is worth £10,000. If he is successful he could earn £30,000 in the next 12 months. He is now rated as No. 1 in England, No. 8 in Europe and 25th in the World. His ambition now is to outplay and out-think the ruling Chinese players so that he can emerge as the unchallengeable No. 1 in the world. He has come a long way in a short time, from being paid £3 a day for an international allowance to his current affluence. The glittering future that lies ahead of him should give him all the success and wealth he wants.

The success formula

This story could be described as a fairytale, with the hero being translated from dirt, dereliction and despair to a fortune, by a good fairy. The good fairy was of his own making, conjured up by utter devotion to his ambition and determination to succeed against all the odds.

The paths that have led John Loveridge and Desmond Douglas to success and wealth can be trod by you with equal success. The formula has been spelt out to you in simple capital letters. All that remains to be said is: 'Go thou, and do likewise!'. Nothing can stop you from reaching your goal if you have the talent, the ambition and the determination to win.

The final case history demonstrates that the ability to perform sheer, good old-fashioned hard work can get you all you want from life. Max Quartermain is a plasterer's mate who had a dream. His ambition was to build and own a *mansion* of his own design and planning. Like so many more successful men before him, he started right at the bottom. He left school without a single 'O' level, and without any idea of what employment he wanted. All he did know was that whatever job he got would be one where he used his hands, because his lack of qualifications would bar him from any job using his brains. He had one golden asset — he could work hard, and fast. It was no big difficulty to get a job as a plasterer's mate, and he soon got the hang of it. He never became a tradesman plasterer, but nobody could touch him as a mate.

His next move was to become self-employed and now, at 36, he can earn more than £400 per week by sheer hard work. By using an outsize hod he can work faster and faster. One day be broke his own record and earned £102 in a single day. He has become known as Britain's No. 1 worker and has lectured to visiting American industrialists on the one subject at which he is a past master — *hard work*! On the way to his dream mansion he was able to buy a house in the stockbroker belt. It had seven bedrooms and all the finest amenities, but was only a stepping stone to his real dream. On the way too, his family had grown to include a wife and three children, but he was able to give them the best of everything, including holidays in places like Barbados costing around £2000.

Then in 1977 his dreams came true after years of planning and a long search for the finest location. He found the right spot in a cul-de-sac overlooking the greens of Stoke Poges golf course. Although it is one of the most desirable plots in the whole of the Thames Valley, it is within easy reach of his home town, Slough. The plot cost £20,500 and the dream mansion will be worth around £100,000. There will be seven double bedrooms, and four bathrooms with gold taps. Downstairs will be a huge elegant lounge, a kitchen with the very latest fitments, and a large games room with billiards tables. Max will do a lot of the building work and plastering himself, and he will landscape the garden. Having sold his existing home for a good figure, he and his family have moved into a flat whilst the work is progressing. In the meantime he has ordered a new Rolls Royce in gold to replace his present Silver Shadow. He hopes the new car will arrive at the same time as his mansion is completed.

His philosophy is very simple. He says: 'There is no particular secret to my success. I got my money fairly and squarely by good old-fashioned hard work. I have an accountant to sort out my income tax, and I always make sure I put enough on one side to pay my tax bills. I know a lot of self-employed people tend to forget about taxes, but that doesn't work. I paid about £6500 in tax last year. A lot of people moan and groan about the state of the country, but there is no escaping the fact that the only way to make money if you're a bloke like me is to work — and work damned hard. It is the only way I could achieve my ambition and build my dream house. There is just one thing I am concerned about. My house will overlook the golf course, but I doubt if I will be allowed to join. After all, I'm only a plasterer's mate.' If you follow in Max Quartermain's footsteps and are successful in a similar way, I hope you will feel happy if the only worry you have is that you aren't reckoned to be good enough socially to join the local golf club.

The American magazine *Fortune* posed the following questions to bosses of companies, particularly to those who, like so many of our top managers, keep their eyes firmly on the ground so that they never notice what is going to happen immediately ahead:

1. Do you find there is no reason to plan your day because as soon as you arrive you know you will be called away on more 'urgent' matters?
2. Are the weekly sales figures the major influence in decision-making? If they are up, does everyone give a sigh of relief? If they are down, does all hell break loose?
3. Is the staff constantly made to stop what it is doing on orders from the top?
4. Do the same emergencies occur again and again because you did not get rid of the underlying causes the first time?
5. Have you been trying to fill a vacancy for months, and is the reason you haven't succeeded that you keep changing the requirements?
6. Do those under you conceal their opinions about you? Do they regard their jobs as being in a rat race, with the rats winning?
7. Is it always difficult for you to tell people where to reach you? Does the telephonist have to tell callers 'I don't know what his plans are for tomorrow (or today, for that matter)?'.
8. Do meetings conclude with a decision that it is premature to do anything at this time, and that the best course is to 'keep our options open'?

9   Do you postpone your holidays because you are constantly having to deal with 'crises'?
10 Did you miss your last health check-up because you were too busy?
11 Does your family think your briefcase grows out of your arm?
12 Do you frequently make, cancel and remake reservations, or appointments?
13 Is it more than a month since you spent a little time thinking about new opportunities.
14 Do you reach decisions that will make you look good today at the expense of tomorrow?

This questionnaire is addressed to managers and bosses. If you are one, then sit up and take notice, for a sincere 'Yes' to anyone of these question means that corrective action has to be taken immediately. If you are on your way to being self-employed and a potential employer, then refer to the questionnaire from time to time to ensure that you don't slip into any of these bad habits. If you are an employee in a firm whose bosses carry on in this fashion, then plan for a change of job. It is simple to take corrective action if you are a guilty boss. Simply reverse the questions!

The basic requirements for success

Business Week posed another set of questions:
1 Do you delegate authority, or do you insist on making every decision yourself?
2 Can you make a firm decision after a reasonable amount of deliberation?
3 Can you take stock of yourself and objectively view your own assets and liabilities?
4 Are you able to listen and learn from others?
5 Are you able to ignore the snide remarks and observations of others, and of unkind critics who would unsurp your position, or undercut you in business?
6 Do you stay reasonably calm and controlled in dealing with crises caused by other people's errors and stupidity?
7 Do you relate on a purely personal level and have at

least two or three good business friends?
8   Are you able to forget the job in favour of your family once the day's work is over?

These questions apply to people at all levels, from the time you start in your first job, to the top men in every sphere. They are absolutely basic. If you answer 'no' to three or more of these questions — and admit that the answer applies over a reasonable length of time — then you need some self-searching, and maybe even some outside help. You may have an emotional problem, or one that you've covered up for years. Executives in particular seem prone to personality disorders — chronic irritability, restlessness, moodiness, preoccupation with food and drink, excessive party-going and heavy smoking. If you are a victim of any one of these, then be warned, you are on the way down, so take action to eliminate whatever disorder you are suffering from.

Tax mitigation

If you are about to start your own business, or become self-employed, you may wonder what the tax situation will be. Here are a few facts which may be reassuring.

Tax assessment is based on the tax year, which starts on 6 April and ends on the following 5 April. Tax on business profits is normally charged on the preceding year, i.e. tax in the tax year 1977/78 is payable on the profits of the business for its financial year ending within the previous tax year — 1976/77.

With a new business, there are obviously no previous year's profits available so there are special provisions for taxing for the first three years. It is possible to avoid tax legitimately by:
1   Taking the option available to be taxed on the *actual* profits in the *second and third* year.
2   Manipulating the closing dates of the financial year accounts, i.e. you are granted the option of choosing a shorter or longer period than 12 months in which to prepare your first set of accounts.

It is therefore possible, with the expert aid of your accountant, to mitigate the burden of tax in your first three years.

This is a very valuable asset to take advantage of during the time you are building up the business and consolidating your position, for every penny you can avoid giving to the taxman can be used to the limit in the business.

When you appoint someone as your accountant, make sure he is familiar with the tax position, so that he can give the advice you will need so very much whilst your business is in the infancy stage. You want to be aware of facts like the above, so that you can keep him on his toes in his work for you. If he doesn't mention the savings that can be made when you first talk to him, but waits for you to ask the questions, it might be an idea to look for a different person to handle your affairs.

Another vital question that you would be wise to ask your accountant and solicitor is 'Would it be advisable for me to register my firm as a limited company, or not?' Only they can give you the best advice after taking into consideration your particular circumstances. Whilst going limited absolves you personally from losing your own assets if the firm has to go into liquidation — and this is the meaning of the phrase 'limited liability' in this connection — there may be reasons why this should not be done at the start of the business, but postponed for later consideration. You must bear this in mind and get answers from your advisors, otherwise you may find that if you are in trouble and could possibly lose everything you have got. Your money, house and every other personal asset can be seized if you go bankrupt, whereas the liquidation of a limited company will at least leave you with your personal goods and chattels. Both states are traumatic, but whilst one can strip you of everything, the other may still leave you something to save from the wreckage and build again.

Launching an invention

If you have an invention you would like to launch, you may find it difficult to get finance for a project that has nothing to recommend it but your fervent conviction that you have a winner. Banks and other conventional lending institutions are not famed for backing dreams. In the past many a fine project has failed, many a wonderful invention has never got further than the drawing board because every possible source of finance refused to lend money to manufacture and market the product. It is a pity that one source of finance has hid its light under a bushel for the 30 years it has been in operation. This is the NRDC (National Research and Development Corporation) with headquarters at 66 Victoria Street, London, SW1. It has around £50 million available for backing promising inventions. Those it has backed in the past must have been successful in the main, because the organisation turned in a profit of £10 million last year. Provided the invention passes the careful scrutiny of its experts and stands a chance in the commercial market, it will pay 50 per cent of the development costs. If the project fails, it will not ask for its money back but, naturally, if you find you have the hoped-for success on your hands, it will take part of the action. Once you have obtained the backing of the NRDC it is not too difficult to get the rest of the money you want from conventional sources.

David Thomson, financial director of NRDC, says the reason why the people in charge of the normal channels of finance are seldom willing to advance money is that they have 'a general lack of confidence'. NRDC has the backing of the government, but is run by people who are neither civil servants nor politically motivated. Businessmen and patent experts run the show, fortunately. When they have helped you to a successful launch of your product and your sales are growing and profitable, you can buy your independence back. It's a pity there aren't more organisations like this for giving assistance to men with ideas for starting a potentially successful business. Last year NRDC invested in as many as 246 inventions, each according to its needs, from a few thousands to over £100,000 for each of some 60 projects.

If you are stuck for more capital on an existing business, an approach to another little-known source of lending might help you out of a difficult financial position. Capital Partners International, of 7c Curzon Street, London W1, will lend as little as £10,000. The source of the finance is a bunch of European businessmen who are interested in backing the good little 'uns of today who can be the big boys of tomorrow. Like the NRDC, they will want a stake in the management. Their help, both in cash and expert management techniques, could be the step you have been looking for to secure success.

Choosing a profitable shop

Some more facts on choosing a potential winner when you are looking for a shop. Every super successful retailer — Marks of Marks and Spencers, Cohen of Tesco, the Sainsburys, and many more right back to Jesse Boot — has based his predictable success on knowing the right place in which to trade. (This has always been given preference over having a flair for the trading itself.) A wrong decision here, and you will undoubtedly fall flat on your face. Check very carefully what the local planning department is doing. Many local authorities will produce, if asked, a plan for the next five or ten years for their area. Usually it is named the Development Plan, and covers the town in which you are interested, as well as all other areas. Rerouting of traffic, proposed pedestrianisation, removal of parking spaces to allow for development, can all affect the flow of shoppers. In 1973, new parking restrictions and one-way systems in Nottingham slashed 30 per cent and more from the turnover of shops in the affected area. Make sure that the spot you have chosen is right for your particular trade, and that there are no local authority restrictions on that trade.

Rent should never be more than 7 or 8 per cent of your turnover if you are trading at a normal gross profit of 30 per cent plus, and proportionately less as your gross profit falls below 30 per cent. If the rent asked breaks that golden rule, then don't try to justify such a figure by kidding yourself you'll soon be achieving a sales figure that will amply cover the rent. Remember, whilst the rent is a fixed figure which won't drop, turnover is pie in the sky so never take a shop where the rent infringes the golden rule.

Whilst the rent is fixed on the floor space, can you use the other space for profit, i.e. the walls, and even the ceiling? Use every inch of wall space to display goods attractively. Many types of food businesses hang goods from the ceiling. A ceiling can be used to hang an angled mirror that can reflect your display and appear to add space visually. Such a mirror can double by acting as a security aid, giving you a bigger and better check on your customers.

It is an established statistical fact that the smaller the town, the larger the percentage of what are known as 'convenience' shops: food, newsagents, takeaways, small cafes, sweets and tobacco. Along with this, the risk is less that the big supermarkets will move in and take your trade. If you choose a shop in a busy road, the best position is near a zebra pedestrian crossing or traffic light. If the area you like has run-down or closed shops, then discard it; there's a reason why the shopping public has deserted it.

Watch your profit margin

If you have an open option concerning which trade you want to operate in, choose the one that has high margins. Many towns seem to have far too many women's dress shops, but they appear to prosper. The only reason is the high gross profit margin at which they operate. By shrewd buying, the owners can make 100 per cent or more on markup from the wholesale or maker's price. They have a quick turnover of stock as well, perhaps 12-15 times a year. This enables them to conserve their valuable capital and to avoid missing out on fashion changes which might otherwise leave them holding stocks that would have to be the subject of a sale.

A service business can be pretty safe and profitable, as few multiples provide facilities in this respect. Machine servicing, launderette, fast shoe repairs, sandwich bar, takeaway, etc.

An executive of one of the biggest supermarket chains, when asked to pick the most profitable small business of the future, opted for the specialist bakers shop, selling better types of bread in many varieties which the supermarkets won't touch as there is no mass market for these. The bread strikes by the employees of the national bakery firms have highlighted the shrewd observation of this executive, for this enabled the small bakeries to cash in on the situation, and to hold on to a lot of valuable new trade. It is a fact that if you are selling the best, you can command the highest price, which in turn means that you benefit from the highest percentage profits. A turnover of £10,000 a year with gross profits of £5000 is far better than a turnover of £50,000 with a gross profit of £5000. You will finish up with a decent net profit in the first case with few headaches, but the second situation will almost certainly show a net loss as overheads will cost more than the gross profit. *Budget for profit, not turnover.*

Communicating effectively

Difficulty in communicating effectively can prejudice good relations with many of the people with whom you have to do business in one way or another. It can in fact lead to a misinterpretation which can prove very costly and embarrassing. You know *what* you want to convey when you speak or write, but you also need to be quite certain that the recipient understands quite clearly what the message is. It is true that a message or statement containing long words and sentences is seldom completely understood, whether it be spoken, telephoned or written. Such messages, because they leave some doubt in the recipient's mind, can lead to action which at the best is slower than required or, at worst, to a totally wrong action. We all know of the continually recurring situation where someone is reproved because they did not carry out an instruction correctly, and their reply is 'I'm sorry, but I thought you said . . . '. The golden rule is first of all to have our own mind perfectly clear on what we wish to convey, then to put it in simple, easily understood language, using short sentences, and without unnecessary elaboration. Always ask yourself 'Can this message be misinterpreted?'.

We all unconsciously ask ourselves when we listen, or read, 'What are the words, and what do they mean?'. When we are in doubt we are left in the position of having to make up our minds what we *think* we have heard or read, and this may be quite different from what the person meant when he spoke or wrote the words and sentences. You can test this theory quite easily. Choose a passage in a newspaper, or book, which you find difficult to understand. Write down what you think it means, then ask three other people what they think it means, and the result will almost certainly be four different interpretations of the passage. We can only have true understanding when our minds react to words with 'Oh yes, I know exactly what that means'.

A young executive in America, fed up with constantly having to deal with 'gobbledegook', coined the phrase KISS which means 'Keep it simple, stupid.' He has a rubber stamp made with the phrase KISS, which he used to stamp on messages and instructions which were not clear in their meaning, and then he sent them back to the originators, who promptly had to get down to rewriting them in simple clear language. If a message was particularly bad, he would use other stamps which were very much to the point. One was BULLSH.., and another RHUBARB. They certainly got action. So do two other things. First train yourself to give clear, simple messages that can be correctly understood, and secondly, deal roughly with people who dish out Rhubarb.

Money-saving tips

One or two tips to save money in your own business:

1   When you send out goods, try and include the invoice in the parcel, instead of sending it separately. That can save a considerable sum in postage over the year.

2   Print on your invoice 'Please pay on this invoice', and only send statements out about twice a year. These can also be included in parcels whenever practicable.

3   Make your payments by credit transfer. The banks encourage this method of paying bills, and will furnish you

with the simple forms free. They do not charge for the
facility, and as many invoices as you wish can be settled with
one cheque. All you have to tell the bank on the form is the
name of the supplier, his bank and bank account number. Your
supplier will furnish these on request when you tell him you
are going to pay by credit transfer.

4   Watch your letter and parcel rates. As they will undoubtedly be changed upwards once again, I will not quote current figures, but it *can* pay to combine two parcels into one and, peculiarly enough, it may sometimes pay to send two parcels instead of one. For instance a parcel of 560 g could cost more than two parcels of 500 g and 60 g respectively.

5   Look into the weight of your packaging. Will one that is lighter do a satisfactory job? Can your correspondence be on a lighter weight paper to cut the cost of letter post? Will a lighter envelope do? Have you looked into the question of lightweight packages which are available for sending small items, or books. Such packages can be bought in an envelope form reinforced with an extremely light plastic interlining. This gives strength and protection whilst being no heavier than an ordinary envelope.

6   Look carefully into the way your telephone is used. The new rules and charges introduced in October 1975 meant that the telephone became one of the major overhead items in a firm's budget. Your telephone dialling code book lists these charges and it will pay you handsomely to study them and take action to minimise the use of the phone in the peak rate hours. Can your calls be confined within the standard or cheap times? *Must* you make calls between 9 a.m. and 1 p.m. Monday to Friday? Remember it costs *50 per cent less* for the same time if you phone after 1 p.m. and if you can phone before 8 a.m. or after 6 p.m. your costs are cut by 75 per cent. This means that for the same money you get 8 min for a local call as against 2 min at peak time, and 3 min for a call up to 56 km as against only 30 sec at peak time. Your trunk call costs could be cut by *as much as five-sixths!* As most telephone calls outside your local area will almost

certainly be higher than postage costs, it will pay to insist that all communications outside the local area should be by letter when they are not urgent.

This will also cut out the wastage of time that invariably goes on during telephone calls. A trunk call lasting 30 min can cost £6. Before making such a call ask yourself if it would pay you to send a letter at a cost of 10p, including the envelope. Get all your outside people who must phone in to restrict their calls to the cheaper times. Check whether your switchboard keeps outside callers hanging on. It may be no skin off your nose, but the callers who are kept waiting *might* be your own outside people, and the switchboard operator's attention to her knitting might cost you a lot of money. Never hang on if the person you want at the other end cannot be found, and the girl on their switchboard wants to start on a marathon call-up around the building. And 'just a minute' can turn out to be 5 or 10 min. Ring off and take one of two options. Either say you will ring again, or ask if the person you want will ring you when he is available. The latter is the cheapest so use it wherever you can. Have you ever thought why the Post Office chose 56 km as a measure of distance for charging? It happens to be exactly 35 miles so it happened to be a handy conversion point, and that's the only reason.

Remunerating salesmen for the best performance

If you employ salesmen, or will shortly expand to the point where you must employ salesmen to sell your goods, what sort of carrot do you use to stimulate their sales effort? The usual methods of paying a salesman fall into three main categories, with variations:
1. *Salary only* About one in four companies pay their salesmen in this fashion and it is becoming more popular; only one in six paid salary only a decade ago.
2. *Salary and bonus* This is used extensively and takes two forms: first, a standard bonus in which every salesman gets the same, and, secondly, a bonus geared to

individual performance. The salesmen themselves naturally prefer the latter.

3   *Salary plus commission*   This, surprisingly enough, is used by the minority of companies, only about one third of the total, but it is, generally speaking, the method of remuneration most favoured by the salesmen themselves.

There is a fourth method, payment by commission only, but it is now very exceptional and usually confined to paying people who are described as 'agents'.

What are the merits of each of the above methods from an employer's point of view? Paying salary and commission can usually generate the best efforts and sales. The salary part should be enough to give the salesman a living wage to cover his basic requirements, and the commission rate should be fixed at a realistic figure from the employer's side. Targets should be achievable, and the commission paid after an acceptable level of sales geared to what your salesman costs you in total with expenses. If a car must be provided then it must be costed in, but don't supply a vehicle which is too cheap, doesn't really do the job, and is not a very good advertisement for your company when your salesmen call upon your customers.

Finally, three rules that ought to be a *must:*

1   Know exactly just how much your salesmen are costing.
2   Know exactly just how much their sales are.
3   Make sure that the yield is worth the cost.

In the earlier chapters of this book, I stressed the use of AIDA as a vital component in selling yourself when seeking a job, or promotion. The same formula was derived, I said, from the world of selling where every salesman worthy of the name uses it to become a success. The Post Office have a booklet available on direct mail featuring this formula. Direct mail can reach your potential customer very efficiently indeed if it is put together right. John Yates, who was commissioned by the Post Office to write the booklet, says the formula, slightly elaborated for this particular purpose, is the key to a good sales letter. AISCDA, as interpreted by John Yates, spells certain success:

Para 1	A	Get *Attention* with the soft-sell approach and mention the product.
Para 2	I and S	Create *Interest* and crisply *Sell* the benefits.
Para 3	C and D	Add *Conviction* (make your message beliveable) and create *Desire* for the product or offer.
Para 4	A	Encourage positive *Action*.

The booklet covers the sales letter all the way from the approach to the final word. It can certainly make the difference between a poor letter that will fail in its purpose, and one which the recipient will like and react favourably to. If your local Post Office doesn't have one in stock, they will get one for you.

Keeping fit

Are you fit? Does your day consist of sleep, work, meals, the telly, and the pub or club? Your fitness depends upon your intake of oxygen, so do something that increases your consumption of this free, but vital, fuel. This is no gimmick, because it has been proved by doctors all over the world that to improve your oxygen capacity to any significant degree will keep you physically well throughout your life. Not only that, but you will find various nagging minor ailments will disappear, and that back-ache in particular will either disappear completely, or be felt just occasionally. The main benefit will be to the heart. When you have trained yourself to increase your intake of oxygen, the heart has to work less, and the pulse rate drops from around 80 at rest, to 60. This means that the heart can cope easily with strenuous bursts of energy without becoming strained.

The exercise you need to accomplish this fitness is simple and easy. Running, even running on the spot, is very good. Start easily and build up gradually until you can run a mile in around 10 min. The muscles of your legs will probably play hell at first, but persevere and by running daily you'll soon be cutting that 10 min to 8 or less. In a week or so you'll radiate a glow of physical health you never dreamt you were capable of. You can either vary the running with something else, or combine it with them. Cycling is an excellent exercise, but you must find a route whereby the effort is sustained, i.e. on fairly level ground. The target is 10 min for a 2-mile ride. Most kids can do this without any trouble at all, so you should find little difficulty in hitting the target. Walking can be combined with running if desired, or taken on its own. The target is 2 miles walking in 30 min, which is an easy target, or 2 miles in 25 min when combined with running.

Why not try cycling or walking to work? Lots of people, including MPs and executives, cycle from the suburbs into the City of London for exercise and usually find they get there quicker than any other form of transport. Swimming is a wonderful sport to increase your oxygen intake and a daily four lengths of a standard pool in 6½ min is an easy target to achieve. Once again, build up to it slowly. So long as you do one or more of these exercises and hit the required target once a day, you'll keep fit and have a long life. To achieve permanent benefit, you must exercise every day. You'll have no difficulty in hitting the target when you are in your 60s and for many years beyond that.

Safeguarding against fraud

When you are in business on your own, or you are a manager, one of the nastiest things you may discover, to your horror, is that you have been the subject of fraud by a trusted employee. Fraud can also affect you if it has been committed on a customer of yours by his employees, for it may embarrass his company financially and your bills don't get paid. It happens at all levels, from fiddling the petty cash to fraud on a gigantic scale. This ancient game of diverting your employer's money into your own pocket takes innumerable forms, and one that has been highlighted recently is that of computer fraud, where the expert operator, knowing full well that the management know nothing about computer working, fiddles the programming so that money is fraudently funnelled into his pocket. Unless there is an auditor who is computer trained and spots the clues to the fraud, the operator goes blithely on without there being any chance of his being found out.

There are a number of warning signals that can spot fraud, and knowing these can enable you to avoid being harmed. First, look for the following in the clients who owe you money:

1. Signs of insufficient working capital or lack of credit, i.e. they always pay late. This may mean just poor management, or it may mean that the firm is being robbed by an employee. No matter what it is, get your money and close the account.
2. Are they in a declining industry where business failures are the order of the day? This may mean delay in paying your accounts, but it can tempt owners to realise all the assets they can and go into liquidation, or bankruptcy.
3. Has a customer a proneness to be at the receiving end of court orders, or lawsuits? Avoid such firms like the plague.
4. Does a firm have a rapid turnover in money managers, e.g. the finance director? This is always a cause for suspicion that there is something very wrong in the management of the company.
5. Does the firm have a sudden rash of special offers, or a sale at a very low price level? Sales and special offers are a necessary part of the selling game, but if they depart from the normal set-up in a company, they usually spell out *trouble*, for the company is obviously trying desperately to convert stock to cash in order to avert a financial disaster.

Avert danger in your own business by adopting methods which show the staff that you are on your toes, and if they step out of line by trying a spot of fraud, they will be found out and punished severely. Taking a pound or so from the petty cash, or till, is outright theft, and if it is not nipped in the bud quickly, it will escalate. Once the culprit realises he can get away with it without suspicion falling upon him, he will have no compunction in repeating the crime for as long as he can and to the maximum he can. Catching him later than sooner usually means a big loss which you can never recover from the culprit. Your books can be fiddled too, and your stock lifted illegally. The only way to minimise these practices, if not cut them out altogether, is to have spot checks at irregular intervals, but never at longer periods than seven days.

Ensure that your daily financing is operating to your satisfaction, so that you know your cash, payments to your suppliers and payments from your customers are in apple-pie order. Whilst the staff handling these may be efficient, never let them be under any misapprehension that you are not in full command of the financial side of the business. Have a rigid system that insists you are supplied with the key financial figures of the business fast and accurately. If you are a one-man business, the possibility of fraud will not arise, but it is vital to the health of the business that you know day-by-day what your financial state is.

Increasing your turnover

If you have a shop there are ways of making people buy from you. Even if you think you are already getting the maximum sales from your pitch, you may still be able to double the turnover by intelligent redesign. You must increase your selling space and reorganise the interior to make sales easier and quicker, and/or attract more customers from the street. A superficial tidying-up is no good. You must look at all the aspects of your shop that you have taken for granted for years. Once you have made the right alterations, you may say to yourself afterwards: 'Why didn't I see that was the obvious thing to do?'.

Part of the Burton Organisation is Peter Robinson whose Top Shops are now the biggest profit-makers in the whole outfit. When they were originally dreamed up, the formula seemed fool-proof. After all, Peter Robinson had a very good name, the shops were in the best shopping spots in towns all over the country as well as London, and the younger generation at which they were aimed were the big spenders. It seemed perfect on paper, yet it all went horribly wrong. They named the project 'Top Shop' and put them on the first floor of some Peter Robinson stores. The choice of clothes offered was terrific, with all kinds of ranges in all kinds of size and colours and from medium to cheap prices. There were juke boxes and snack bars to draw the young people. What actually happened was the exact opposite of the paper success. The management soon found what should already have been known, that the floors above the ground only do a fraction of the business done just inside the ground-floor doors. Those potential young customers who did penetrate to the first floor found themselves confused and overwhelmed by the vast choice. The place was also hot and noisy with the juke boxes and the displays were crowded, making it difficult for people to browse comfortably. The result was that one-third of the clothes were never sold, and had to be jobbed off at a big loss.

That brought the management sharply to their senses, and they rethought the whole job. Having learnt their lesson the hard way, they came up with a new winning formula:

1 *Concentrate* Instead of offering a big quantity of low-priced clothes, they now offer better-quality goods at higher prices, giving a bigger mark-up.
2 *Clarify* The display is divided into special areas, with skirts, coats, etc., separate from each other. Each area is colour coded so that the shopper can find exactly what she wants easily.
3 *Control* They have specialist boutiques inside the shop, but controlled by themselves instead of the manufacturer, as it was before. This goes for everything they now sell. They retail, and the manufacturer makes to their order without interfering with the retail displays.
4 The Top Shop is now made attractive by making features out of the make-up of the floor itself, such as the escalators.
5 *Comfort* The signs are now simple and easily followed, so customers move around without confusion. Air conditioning has been installed to reduce the heat and make shopping comfortable.

Summarising the lessons for any shopkeeper, large and small: Provide for the business you are in, *don't* stock items that are out of the strict range you should be selling. Attract shoppers to every area of the shop by clear signs. If you work on more than one floor, make the stairs or escalators work for you by inviting people to use them with enticing displays and adverts for the floor above. Check your lighting, temperature and ventilation to get the most comfortable atmosphere. Shoppers will not return to a shop where they get hot and bothered. Make your window display arresting and let it lead the eye to the interior of the shop. Fewer and fewer shops still have backs to their windows; the display, window and interior, is totally integrated to make the biggest impact. Give your shop personality by careful display, attractive assistants in well designed clothes, your stationery and vans carefully designed to catch the eye and enhance your prestige. Some people have turned a poor, failing store into one that is booming by using the simple theme 'trade-up and dress-up'. It works every time. Fuse that theme with the new Top Shop formula of the four Cs — Concentrate, Clarify, Control and Comfort, and you should be laughing all the way to the bank.

Successful expansion

After you have started your own business and got it on its feet, there will come a time when you will want to expand. Such a move usually means that you want more finance but there are many pitfalls in your path when you set out to persuade money sources to make a loan available. Your accountant can supply you with figures showing that an expansion can be a profitable venture, but there are precautions you must take which are out of the accountant's province, and for which you alone can be responsible. Think the proposed venture over in very great detail. The loan must make complete commercial sense, otherwise it merely becomes a burden you'll never get off your back. Do not give a pennyworth more security than you have to, to justify getting the loan, and make sure that the loan can be repaid when you are able. Some loans specify a number of years over which they can be repaid. Make sure there is an escape clause in case you can pay off the loan earlier, for you don't want to be saddled with paying interest for the full term. Read the small-print clauses and make sure you don't give away more money than you have to.

Assess the longest period for which you may want the loan, then borrow for that period. It is suicidal to borrow for a short period in the *hope* that you can pay off the capital and the interest in that time. You'll be sunk if your optimism is confounded. Whatever you do, get the maximum flexibility built into the loan agreement. The clauses may look very fine at the outset, but may be quite onerous in five years' time when circumstances have changed. Don't borrow a penny more than is absolutely necessary, and keep your borrowings well within your total asset value. On the other hand it is better to work with borrowed money than to live off your debtors and creditors, as pointed out in an earlier chapter. In the long run, financial discipline must be the order of the day. Force yourself to work within your financial constraints whilst at the same time keeping a tight hold on the basic efficiencies of the business.

Getting to the buyer

Getting to the man who can buy can prove to be a difficult proposition to anyone who is just starting up in business. It can be just as difficult to a salesman who is pioneering a new territory, but there are a number of tried and proven ways of contacting the man who can give an order. If it is a new area, then a bit of geographical homework will provide much basic information. Area sales maps' of the country can be bought which pinpoint the most likely areas for profitable sales campaigns. Once you know the best areas to concentrate on, you have to find the names and addresses of the firms you wish to interest in your products. The telephone *Yellow Pages* trade directories are first-class for this purpose. They are as up-to-date as any other type of register, with the entries under trade or professional headings, so a list of firms can soon be made.

Trade directories are not very accurate. Entries may only be made if firms have paid for them. It may be two or three years after the information has been supplied before publication date. Chambers of Commerce keep a register of their members and usually of the principal of each member firm. Reference books like *Dun and Bradstreet, Kompass* and *Kellys* give essential information that might be necessary, such as financial details, names of directors, etc.

Once you have a comprehensive list of names and addresses, you can start contacting them. If you want the name of the person who can buy, then request this by telephone, or get your salesman to obtain the necessary information. Follow up with direct mail to introduce your firm and products to the buyer. Advertise in the appropriate trade journals and newspapers. Appointments can be made on the telephone for calls by your salesman. He will need the following information: Name, address and telephone number of the prospective customer; time and date of appointment; name and position of the person to be seen; any 'inside' information, such as size of company, is it part of a bigger Group?; how the contact was made (direct mail, answer to advert, phone, etc.). The rest is up to him. He should phone to confirm the appointment, just saying who he is and the firm he represents, and 'I would like to discuss . . . (the product's name without going into any details). May I confirm X a.m. or p.m. for the appointment?' Don't discuss anything further with the buyer on the phone, or he may be given the opportunity of making up his own mind to reject the approach.

Once you are face-to-face with the buyer remember he expects you to try and sell him your product. This is not so daft as it may sound. One buyer for a large company said that only about one in ten salesmen actually tried to sell to him, the others expected him to evaluate the product for themselves and then expected an order.

SUMMARY

What are the final truths of success? They can be summed up, perhaps, in a few simple sentences. The person who knows his real abilities, and gives of his best for himself and for those around him, will achieve true success and be a living proof of what true success means to all those he contacts. By continually analysing your achievements and concentrating on those areas in which you know you can succeed, all your dreams can come true and all your goals reached. One of your greatest satisfactions will be the realisation that there is no ceiling to your achievements. The infinite is the limit provided you remain true to yourself and your talents.

When you have a job to do, the surest way to prove yourself, and set your feet firmly on the way upward, is to concentrate on the job, carry out all the assigned tasks and achieve whatever targets have been set for the jobs in which you are engaged or which you control. Set your sights on increasing production, reducing costs, carrying out allotted programmes efficiently. Give concrete evidence that you are working hard and efficiently above the norms set. Let it be seen that your performance goes beyond whatever can be plotted as average on a chart.

Success leads to greater success, but never be complacent, for there is no ultimate triumph. A higher peak always looms beyond the one you have just vanquished. Discard the traditional concepts of success and do not allow yourself to be diverted from the path you have plotted for yourself. There is nothing constant about business, but opportunity is always there ready to be seized by the man who has trained himself to use his talents. The trained, all-round man will always come out top against any competition. Success for such a man becomes a happy habit.

All the lessons in this book can be condensed into a few words. What they do is to exhort you to apply simple commonsense to whatever you undertake. Keep it simple, and tackle it the commonsense way. There's really nothing more to it than that. Keep your brain uncluttered by committing to paper as much as you can, and then you can take action to the limit of your abilities.

Success with happiness will be yours — the final great attainment.

INDEX

Action, make the prospect want to take, 24-6
Advice, taking professional, 118-19
Age is not always a bar, 57
Aggression, avoidance of, at interviews, 36
AIDA:
    formula of salesmanship, 24-6
    system of, and interviews, 32-3
A-Levels, some detractions of, 9
Appearance, importance smart, 24
Application, letter of, for first job, 28
Application forms:
    a tip about, 34-5
    how to surmount the barriers of, 45-59:
        always add your own resumé, asked to or not, 52-5
        age should not be allowed to go against you, 57-8
        analysis of the form, 48-9
        applicant must bring in desire, interests and objectives as well as enterprise somehow and show he can think creatively, 52-5
        apply the AIDA system, 52-3
        criticism of system, 51
        drawbacks of, 46-7
        dwells on the past not future, 46
        emphasise facts to support your claim, 58
        employers, like customers, do not always know exactly what they want, 58
        paraphrase and précis your previous jobs, 59
        resumé, what it must contain, 56-9
Aptitude tests, 34
Assets, what are your personal?, 8-9
Association of Small Businesses, help from, 110
Attention, arouse people's, 24-6
Attributes:
    checklist of, 93
    listing and grading your, 91-5
Average, being above the, 90-1

Bad debts, 119-122
Big-headedness, nothing wrong with, 12
Boss, see only the, when you want a change, 27
Brain, illimitable capacity of, 11

Brown, David John, the story of 96-7
Budgeting is a must, 124
Business, running your own:
  aids to assure success in, 142-65:
    AIDA system to be invoked, 157-8
    basic needs, 147-8
    buyer, getting in contact with, 164-5
    case histories, 142-7
    communicating, importance of satisfactorily, 153-4
    directories, trade, 164-5
    expansion, success for, 163-4
    fitness, mental and physical, 158-9
    fraud, 159-61
    invention, how to launch, 149-51
    'KISS — Keep it Simple, Stupid', 154
    location, 152
    money-saving tips, 154-6
    National Research and Development Corporation, address of, and help from, 150-1
    phone costs, cutting down on, 156
    postage, reducing the bill for, 154-6
    profit margins, keeping a watch on, 152-3
    rent, correct ratio for, 152
    salesmen, paying by results, 156-7
    space, maximum utilization of, 152
    tax mitigation, 148-9
    theft, 159-61
    turnover, increasing your, 161-3
    what to avoid, 146-7
  buying, as a going-concern, 130-9, 151-2
    checklist, cold appraisal of, 131-6
    dealing with agents, 137
    failure, safeguards against, 131-6
    financial structure, daily monitoring of, 136-7
    overheads, 138-9
    profit potential must exist, 139
    what to guard against, 130-1
  overcoming starting up problems, 117-29:
    bad debts, and their recovery, 119-22
    bad payers, 122
    budgeting, 124
    credit control, 119-22
    customers, finding the, 126-9
    distributorships, 122-3
    insurance, 118
    legislation, 117-18, 124-6
    maintaining good relations, 122-4
    overtrading, mistake of, 123
    paying the bills, 122-4
    purchasing policy, 129
    salesmanship, technique of good, 127-9
    taking professional advice, 118-19
    VAT, 124-6
  planning has to be simple, 111
  starting, 96-116:
    approach, 96-7
    capital, operating on a small, 111-13
    exploiting the success of others, 113-16
    good idea, pursuit of a, 98
    help, where to get official, 109-111
    market, finding the gaps in, 105-7
    plunge, taking the, 102-5
    preparation is vital, 100-2
    profiting from leisure, 98-100

Capital:
  and your own business, 107-9, 111-13
  sources for raising, 150-1
Career advice, Education Departments', 67-8
Case at interview, state yours with confidence, 26

Cash, operating on a basis of paying, 113
Categories of job-hunters, 1
Change:
    be prepared for, 26-8
    jobs and the world today under the circumstances of, 83-95
    proper way to make a, 27
Checklist when buying own business, 131-6
Civil Service entry for women, 43
Clark, Tom, example of determination by, 105-7
Commodity, finding and matching a low-priced, with market demand, 114
Communicating, importance of satisfactorily, 153-4
Competition, facing up to, 23
    used as a driving force, 85-6
Complacency a bar to progress, 2-3
Concept, employer looks for a person selling a, 57
Conclusions of this study, 166-7
Conduct at interviews, 31-2
Confederation of British Industry, help from 109
Confidence at interviews, 31-2
Conformity inhibits, 9
COSIRA, help from, 104
Council for Small Industries in Rural Areas, help from, 104
Credit control, 119-22
Customer relations, vital need to maintain, 97
Customers, finding business, 126-9

Dartflights, success of business from making of, 98
Dead-end jobs, 88
Degree, does it sometimes inhibit?, 9
Delivery on time, 114
Desire, arousing a person's, 24-6
Determination a must, 3
Directories, trade, 164-5
Discounts, taking advantage of, 113

Disloyalty is NOT always a prime factor, 27
Distributorships, 122-3
Dress, importance of smart, 24
Drive, having personal, 10-11
Drivers, women as, 37-8

Economic climate, exploiting the, 102
Edenlite, example of exploiting gap in market, 105
Edison, Thomas Alva, 5
Editorial publishing posts for women, 41
Einstein, Albert, 13
Employees, 75% fail to use best abilities, 83-4
Employer:
    essential to play fair with, 22-3
    getting an understanding of a prospective, 33-4
    what is he looking for?, 24-6
Employer and shopper have a similar outlook, 24-6
Employment Offices, jobs through, 33
Employment Protection Act, effects of, 22-3
English, careless approach to, 21
Entertainment business, 99
Enthusiasm a basic need, 10-11
Estate agents, how to handle, 137
Expansion of business, successful, 163-4

Factories, rent-free, 104
Farmwork, attributes for, 20
Fay, Philip, 6-7
Female aspects of job acquisition, 37-44
Finance for own business, 103-4
    daily check on, 136-7
Firms, advantages of changing, 26-8
Fitness, mental and physical, 158-9
Formula for own successful business, 99-100
Fraud prevention, 159-61
Frustration, causes of, 9

Going-concern, buying a, *see under* Business

Gower, Philip, success story of, 111-13

Handwritten applications are best, 29
Happiness is the only goal, 84-5
Help, where to get official, 109-11

ICFC, help from, 104
Ideas for your own business, 96-8
Industrial and Finance Corporation, loans from, 104
Industrial change, effects of, 81-2
Industry, women in heavy, 37-8
Inputs and outputs, VAT, 125-6
Insurance for own business, 118
Interest, arousing people's, 24-6
Interviewers, what goes through their minds, 33-5
Interviews:
  dress and appearance vital at, 24
  how to get a personal, 34-5
  how to succeed at:
    aggression is a fault, 64
    answer question simply but emphatically, 65
    avoid mannerisms, 64
    be confident and natural, 63
    be succinct, 64
    bluffing will be seen through, 63
    clear up uncertainties, 65
    do not monopolise conversation, 64
    don't ask if 'you stand a chance', 66
    ensure you make all your points, 66
    eye-contact, 63
    familiarity is frowned upon, 64
    gently ease initiative your way, 65
    if interviewer shows antagonism, make as if to go, 65
    interviewer, what impresses, 63
    keep it on a pleasant exchange basis, 60
    keep to the point, 64
    keep your cool, 65
    nervousness will exist on both sides, 60
    planning counter-tricks, 62-3
    reasons for failure, 61
    seven essential aspects summarised, 69
    tricks used by interviewers, 61-2
    uncertain outcome should mean you should start looking elsewhere, 66
    your conduct at, 63
  preparation beforehand, 32-3, 34-5
Inventions, how to launch, 149-51
Inventors, example of attitude of, 4
Investment, are you a good, to your employer?, 27

Jobs:
  application letter for the first, 28
  typical attributes for, 93-4
Job applications, dress and appearance vital at, 24
Job-hunters, five categories of, 1

Legislation and own business, 117-18, 124-6
Leisure, making a profit from, 98-100
List what you are good at, 8
Literature, business, 126-7
Letters of application, specimen, 28-31:
Loans, where to get, 104-5
Location of business, 152

Manager, requirements for job as, 19
Market, finding the gaps in the, 105-7
Marriage and the career woman, 42
Middlemen, 115
Mistakes, forget past, as an irrelevance, 3-4
Money-saving tips, 154-6

My Way (Song by Sinatra) is a good summary of success formula, 95

National Research and Development Corporation, address of, and help from, 150-1
Need, providing a, 107

Objectives:
 set and keep to, 3
 the key word of success, 56-7
Opportunity:
 being one step ahead to seize an, 26
 creating your own, 16-36:
  three examples of how to, 17-20
Outputs, VAT, 125-6
Overheads, managing one's, 138-9
Overtrading, mistake of, 123
Overwork equals inefficiency, 116

Patience, women's need for, 39
Peachey, Louise, 40
Perseverence, women's need for, 39
Persistence towards chosen objectives is paramount, 56
Planning your own business, 100-2
Plans for business need to be simple, 111
Pluck, women's need for, 39
Plunge, taking the, woman and, 41
Postage, reducing bills for, 154-6
Potential, understanding your own, 86-9
Prejudice against women, 42
Premises for own business, 103
Presentation of your 'package' as as a person to be attractive, 25
Price must be right, 114
Product (yourself), selling the, 24-6
Professional advice, taking, 118-19
Professional and Executive Recruitment Scheme, 44, 68

Profit margins, keeping a watch on, 152-3
Promotion:
 seeking, 70-80:
  avoid confusing self-confidence with arrogance, 78
  do not aim too low, 76
  enterprise, methods used to stifle one's, 72-3
  four steps to decide when ready for, 74-5
  get your superior on your side, 75
  keep your performance in writing, 76
  making yourself a desirable 'package', 72
  'Management by Exception' concept, 73
  'Management by Inertia' concept, 73-4
  moving elsewhere, 74
  obstacles, overcoming the, 78-80
  occasions when to by-pass your manager, 77-8
  problems when newly promoted, 79-80
  reasons against, 70-1
  regimentation, is it desirable?, 71-2
  savings you can make for company must be more than your own salary, 77
  seeking an interview with the key man, 78
 when ways to, are blocked, 16-17, 23-4
'P's, the three women's, 39
Purchasing policy in own business, 129

Question whatever you hear, 4

Redundancy:
 a problem for women, 43-4
 through change, 81-2
Relatives, recommendation of employed, 22
Relax, ability to, 116
Rent-free factories, 104

Rent of premises, correct ratio for, 152
Rippin, Robin, 10
Risks, taking sensible, 99

Safe jobs, insecurity of, today, 81-2
Salesmanship, technique of good, 24-6, 127-9
Salesmen, paying by results, 156-7
Satisfaction, what gives you the most?, 10
Secretary, requirements of a, 18
Security in a fast-changing world, 81
Self-discovery of good points, 7-9
Self-help, 7-9
Self is the only bar to success, xi-xii
Selling yourself, how to go about, 24-6
Shops, buying as a going-concern, see under Business
Sinclair, Dr Michael, 104-5
Single-mindedness, 98
Skilled work, women in, 38-9
Small Business Bureau, help from 110
Small Firms Information Centres, 110
Space, maximum utilization of, 152
Sport as a source of business, 99
Stamped addressed envelopes to be sent with letters of application, 29
Stock-broker, women as, 40-1
Striking out on your own, 96-116
Study, conclusion of this, 166-7
Success:
    breeds success, 11-12
    business exploitation of others', 113-16
    is in the mind, xii
    still leaves for further potential, 85
    summary of what is, 166-7
    the seven foundation stones of, 56-9

Talents:
    be honest about your own, 20-1
    discovering your marketable, 1-3
    how to discover your, 6-15
    is always latent, 13
    relating your, to a new job, 94-5
Tax mitigation, 148-9
Telephone, cutting costs of, 156
Theft, prevention of, 159-61
Tradition, need to break with, 4, 10-11
Transport, controlling the ever-increasing costs of, 108
Turnover, how to increase your, 161-3

Unfair dismissal, 22-3
Union of Independent Companies, 109
Up-to-date, keeping yourself, 89-90

VAT, 124-6

Walker, Eric, 6-7
Weeding-out process, 34-5
Women:
    are as good as men, 41
    job-getters, 37-44
    prejudice against, 39
    work of, the traditional, 38
'Workoholics', 116

Yellow Pages, using the, 104, 110, 164